OODGEROO: A Tribute

AUSTRALIAN LITERARY STUDIES

EDITOR: *L.T. Hergenhan*

ASSISTANT EDITOR: *Martin Duwell*

EDITORIAL ASSISTANT: *Irmtraud Petersson*

EDITORIAL ADVISERS: *Geoffrey Dutton, A.D. Hope, A.N. Jeffares, Joseph Jones, Frank Kermode, Brian Kiernan, Leonie Kramer, R.L. McDougall, J.P. Matthews, Bede Nairn, Michael Roe, G.H. Russell, Michael Wilding, G.A. Wilkes, Judith Williams.*

EDITORIAL COMMITTEE: *Alan Lawson, Stan Mellick, Chris Tiffin, Helen Tiffin, Graeme Turner.*

1995 PRICES (postage *included for all*) are as follows: Annual Subscription: Aust: individuals and school libraries A$27.50; institutions A$38.50. Overseas: individuals A$33.00, institutions A$45.00. Available back issues: prices on

BUSINESS CORRESPONDENCE should be addressed to:
Australian Literary Studies
c/- The Manager, Journals Division
University of Queensland Press
PO Box 42, St Lucia Q 4067 Australia
Phone: (07) 365 2606
Fax: (07) 365 1988

EDITORIAL CORRESPONDENCE should be addressed to:
Professor L.T. Hergenhan, Editor
Australian Literary Studies
Department of English
University of Queensland Q 4072 Australia
Fax: (07) 365 2799; Phone: (07) 365 1419

CONTRIBUTIONS: *Australian Literary Studies* follows the *MLA Handbook* Second or Third Edition (1984, 1988) for matters of presentation, using parenthetical documentation and a list of works cited. However, single inverted commas are used for quotations. Contributions should be typescript (double-spaced), and content footnotes should be numbered consecutively. Length of contribution is up to 5,000 words for articles, 2,000-3,000 words for notes. The copies should be sent and return postage enclosed. Contributors are asked to indicate whether a final (revised) version of accepted material could be provided on floppy disc.
The minimum payment is $90 for articles, $60 for reviews.

Australian Literary Studies is published with the aid of grants from the Literature Board of the Australia Council for the Arts.

ISSN 004 9697

OODGEROO

A Tribute

A special issue of Australian Literary Studies
Volume 16, No. 4

Guest Editor: Adam Shoemaker

Associate Editor: Laurie Hergenhan

Editorial Assistant: Irmtraud Petersson

Australian Literary Studies
University of Queensland Press

First published 1994 by University of Queensland Press
Box 42, St Lucia, Queensland 4067 Australia

Typeset by ATA Typesetters, Brisbane
Printed in Australia by McPherson's Printing Group

Distributed in the USA and Canada by
International Specialized Book Services, Inc.,
5804 N.E. Hassalo Street, Portland, Oregon 97213–3640

Publication of this title was assisted by
the Commonwealth Government through
the Australia Council, its arts funding
and advisory body.

Sponsored by the Queensland Office
ARTS QUEENSLAND of Arts and Cultural Development.

Cataloguing in Publication Data
National Library of Australia

Oodgeroo a tribute.

1. Noonuccal, Oodgeroo, 1920–   . — Biography. 2.
Noonuccal, Oodgeroo, 1920–   . Criticism and interpretation.
3. Women authors, Australian — 20th century — Biography.
[4]. Aborigines, Australian — Women — Biography. 5.
Australian literature — Aboriginal authors — Biography. I.
Shoemaker, Adam, 1957–   .

A821.3

ISBN 0 7022 2800 1

Contents

Illustrations

Acknowledgments

This collection, both a special issue of *Australian Literary Studies (ALS)* and a book, would not have been possible without the endorsement of Denis Walker, Lucy Pettit and other members of the family of Oodgeroo of the Tribe Noonuccal, Custodian of the Land Minjerriba. The editors of *ALS* and its publishers wish to thank them for their support and encouragement.

In February 1994 a trust was established to carry on the work of Oodgeroo, with the aim of achieving a just reconciliation between Aboriginal and non-Aboriginal people. Those involved with the writing, editing and publication of this volume support that goal. Accordingly, it has been decided to share the royalties from the sale of this book between the "Oodgeroo of the Noonuccal Tribe, Custodian of the Land Minjerriba Trust" and *ALS*, a journal subsidised by the Literature Board of the Australia Council. Thanks are due to all contributors for endorsing this course of action. The editors of this volume, as is customary with *ALS*, have worked in an unpaid capacity.

I would also like to acknowledge the pivotal role of Professor Laurie Hergenhan who, as editor of *ALS* and associate editor of this volume, suggested its original concept and has given it unstinting support throughout the editing process. I am also grateful to Dr Irmtraud Petersson, Editorial Assistant of *ALS*, for seeing the book through the press, and to Ms Angela Tuohy, for her typing and secretarial assistance.

For permission to reproduce photographs and illustrations I am grateful to Ulli Beier, Jim Clayden, Kathie Cochrane, Rhonda Craven, Branco Gaica, Chris Marr, Caroline Turner and Patricia Walker.

Finally, I wish to thank the English Department, University of

Queensland; the School of Humanities, Queensland University of Technology; and the UFR d'Anglais of the University of Toulouse-Le Mirail for the use of essential facilities.

Adam Shoemaker

Introduction

This book owes its existence to a person, a place and an event. That person was Oodgeroo of the Noonuccal Tribe, Custodian of the Land Minjerriba.

The place — Minjerriba — appears on Australian maps as North Stradbroke Island, and lies twenty minutes by boat off the eastern coast of Queensland, due east of Brisbane. It is known to most Australians as a holiday island, renowned for its natural beauty, its whales and dolphins, its fresh-water lakes, its surfing, fishing and swimming.

But the island is also used for other purposes: the sand-mining conglomerate, Consolidated Rutile, has had a major operation on the island for many years. There are schools, churches and a permanent community in Dunwich, as well as the towns of Amity and Point Lookout, which boasts one of the most spectacular ocean views in Australia. Most important, Minjerriba is home to Aboriginal people of various tribes — as it has been for centuries. And many of those Black Australians are extremely active in organisations on the island, working tirelessly to improve the level of Aboriginal housing, education and health in the community.

One of the most prominent of these workers was Oodgeroo.

It was in September 1920 that Oodgeroo, as Kath Walker, was born on this island. She spent her formative years there and returned to live permanently on a small property called "Moongalba" in 1970, establishing it as one of the most important initiatives in Aboriginal education ever seen in Australia. Over nearly a quarter of a century, 30,000 visitors — both Aboriginal and non-Aboriginal — visited Oodgeroo, learned about Black Australian culture; tasted traditional foods; camped on the sand; and both heard and told stories of the land.

Many — but not all — were children. There were students, former prisoners, journalists, foreign visitors, business people, reformed drug addicts, musicians, painters, poets and fellow Black Australians of all ages. All came to learn and all left wiser — and many of their voices are in this book.

Thus, Oodgeroo, her achievements and the perspectives on her life which appear in this collection, cannot be divorced from the land of which she was so much a part. That is why this collection of essays pays homage to the land Minjerriba as well as to the uniqueness of Oodgeroo.

This returns us to the day which sparked the creation of this volume. On Thursday 30 September 1993, a unique event took place on the island. Called the ''Minjerriba Tribute'' it was a national celebration of Black Australian authors, the largest such gathering ever to take place in Queensland. It featured Aboriginal writers and storytellers from every state and territory of the country, music, traditional foods, workshops, book launches and speeches. Oodgeroo had been a driving force behind the Tribute; when the idea for it had been put to her in November 1992 she simply replied: ''Fantastic — let's do it!''.

But, as the date of the Tribute approached, Oodgeroo's health worsened — quite rapidly — and her death on 16 September came as a huge shock. The waves and ripples of her passing were felt all over Australia as they were in many other countries. And while thousands of people mourned her death the question arose: ''Should the Minjerriba event be cancelled, out of respect to Oodgeroo and her family?'' And an answer came back, almost as quickly: ''No, but the character of the day will change: it will become a tribute to the life's work of Oodgeroo, to her land — and to all Aboriginal authors.''

The day itself, two weeks later, was marvellous: it was one of the most memorable of festivals. Every one of the hundreds of participants rejoiced in Oodgeroo's life and inspiration and, above all, in the range of her achievements. In turn, out of the Minjerriba Tribute arose the idea for this volume: a collection of essays providing various perspectives on Oodgeroo of the Tribe Noonuccal, in all her inspirational variety.

Minjerriba is also the central theme in my own relationship with Oodgeroo. My first contact with her took place on her island, the place of her birth, as did my last contact with her — over fourteen years later, on the day of her funeral. In those years, I was fortunate to visit her dozens of times at Moongalba, her "sitting-down place", a strong centre of Aboriginality.

I never visited her alone, nor did I ever find her alone. Whether it was groups of students, overseas visitors or family members, she always seemed to be surrounded by people. As she often used to say, "Everyone wants a piece of me" — and no wonder. She had an uncanny ability to make every person who sat on her front porch feel totally welcome. I have seen normally voluble university vice-chancellors practically struck dumb by Oodgeroo, simply enjoying her wise presence. There were visiting authors too — hushed as much by the tranquillity of Moongalba as by her trenchant wit.

The Canadian novelist and short-story writer, Audrey Thomas, said at the time of her visit that she found her afternoon at Moongalba "unforgettable". Oodgeroo seemed to know exactly when a sea-eagle would swoop down for its food; when a kookaburra would call; when the wind would gently blow one of her many carpet-snake wind-sculptures. And she was always the soul of generosity, offering a cup of tea to students, regaling them with stories of her exploits with hijackers, thieves and politicians.

But it was when she spoke to children that Oodgeroo excelled herself. I will never forget her involvement in a project to encourage primary school students from all over Queensland — both Aboriginal and non-Aboriginal — to express themselves in verse. As voices crackled over a telephone transponder, Oodgeroo's inspiration of the younger generation became palpable. A humorous six-word poem came in from an Aboriginal boy in Boulia, in the far west of the state:

Basketball —
Smelly
Dirty
Sweaty
Bouncy —
Basketball!

Oodgeroo loved it. "That's wonderful!" she enthused; "now you listen to your parents and teachers when they tell you what to do — won't you? Don't forget: knowledge is power — now go out and *get some*!'' For me, this encapsulated Oodgeroo's special gift: her capacity to rise or descend to any level in order to communicate as an equal. She was always able to establish that contact — figuratively and practically speaking, to place her hand on your arm for emphasis. In this way, Oodgeroo always believed that knowledge was power; her life was proof of the power of Black Australian knowledge and insight.

Obituaries tell only one story about Oodgeroo's life, as complimentary as they may be. After all, the genre of "the eulogy" is itself a highly stylised literary art-form. As a result, the catalogue of achievements which her life represented can become abstracted and distant from the character of Oodgeroo herself. Oodgeroo was a woman who abolished boundaries; her life and career defy simple biographical listings.

But she has often been represented as being something quite different — a poet of the people — as if such a person is born rather than made. But, as she pointed out as long ago as in 1977:

> You could say a poet is born, but you're not born a poet. You have to work on it ... I felt poetry would be the breakthrough for the Aboriginal people because they were storytellers and song-makers, and I thought poetry would appeal to them more than anything else. It was more of a book of their voices that I was trying to bring out, and I think I succeeded in doing this.[1]

Again, the word "voices" is crucial. Whether spoken, sung, recited or recorded, Oodgeroo's voices were plural and diverse. Therefore, although she was in one way the best-known Aboriginal person of her generation, in another sense this was not so. As long as she is thought of simply as a "Black Australian poet" — as crucial as her contribution was in this area — the many-sidedness of Oodgeroo will remain invisible. And this would be a terrible irony for one who gave so much of her life to the public.

This is not to down-play the significance of Oodgeroo's verse. Its impact has been felt, both in original versions and in translation, all over the world. A number of contributors to this collection — such as Eve Fesl and Bob Hodge — recognise her absolute importance to the artistic and political processes of Black Australian poets. At the same time, they both call into question accepted theories and critical responses to her verse. Hodge, in particular, challenges the methods employed by many academics to dissect the poetry of Oodgeroo, preferring instead to see her verse as a highly strategic and unified body of work.

Others — such as Eva Rask Knudsen and Anne Brewster — take up this theme by concentrating on the panoply of Oodgeroo's poetry and its centrality to the Aboriginal oral tradition of storytelling. Both examine theories of postcolonialism and link them, in different but fascinating ways, with the role of Oodgeroo as an independent female spokesperson and artist. Rask Knudsen's Danish perspective contrasts here — in a very stimulating way — with that of many Australian critics.

Still others, such as Mudrooroo, discuss Oodgeroo's verse only to reject the notion that she ever really saw herself as a poet. His challenging essay seeks also to break down barriers between polemical and other forms of writing, so that a new way of reading Oodgeroo's work can emerge.

Internationalism is a salient theme in many of these essays, as it was in Oodgeroo's own life. For example, Nicholas Jose brings together cultural history, bilateral relations with the People's Republic of China and an innovative interpretation of Oodgeroo's Chinese poems. His comprehensive account of Oodgeroo's 1986 visit to that country sheds a whole new light upon her overseas role as a "defiant diplomat". Then, from a Scottish perspective, Angela Smith further expands our understanding of Oodgeroo's internationalism (and universalism). By focussing comparatively upon her work and that of the Jamaican poet, Louise Bennett, she provides a lucid image of two writers whose highly politicised pride in heritage and gender informs their literary achievements.

A number of important essays highlight Oodgeroo's crucial contribution as an educationalist. By concentrating upon this aspect of Oodgeroo's career over different periods of time, Alan Duncan and Rhonda Craven offer interpretations of her educative role which are as complementary as they are illuminating. At the same time the sense of intimacy which is spoken into being by Rhonda Craven is a testament to the dramatic effect which Oodgeroo had upon so many young Australians in the classroom. As a Sydney student who worked closely with Oodgeroo for the last three years of her life, Kristie Lorenz, recently put it:

> She was the most admirable and wisest person I have ever known. I still have some trouble believing she is gone ... But then I realised that she has given her contribution to Australia and it is now up to us to continue in her work ... Oodgeroo's favourite saying is also one of mine: "Evil will only triumph when good men choose to do nothing."[2]

Such highly personal relationships were paramount for Oodgeroo — and they are reflected in many of these essays. The collection opens with a poignant story of Oodgeroo's childhood, written by her sister Lucy Pettit. Later, Philip McLaren pays tribute to Oodgeroo as a stimulus for his own successful career as an author, and describes his unforgettable meeting with her at Brisbane's Warana Writers' Week. Roberta B. Sykes shares a moving and singular portrait of Oodgeroo as a fellow Black Australian activist over many years, as a mentor and as a friend. Then, Oodgeroo's longtime publisher and ally, John Collins, offers an affectionate and perceptive view of their decades of collaboration. Finally, the evocative message of the Darug people — represented by Pat Jarvis, Fay Richards and Edna Watson — acknowledges their debt to Oodgeroo, as an Aboriginal leader who is loved, respected and sorely missed.

The extreme variety of Oodgeroo's achievements is underlined in the remaining contributions. For example, Robert Tickner's essay discusses the pivotal role which she played in the arena of Australian federal politics, especially in the final decade of her career. As he relates the story of Oodgeroo's considerable talents as a visual artist, Ulli Beier also sheds light on her political skills, her art work, her tenacity and her irrepressible sense of humour.

The final two essays in the collection — those of Sue Rider and myself — adopt the wider perspective of theatrical performance. In her piece, Rider gives a detailed account of Oodgeroo's significant impact upon the Australian theatre. What is particularly interesting is Rider's treatment — from a director's point of view — of the challenges and successes of working with Oodgeroo on the dramatisation of her poetry. Finally, my own contribution reads the concept of "performance" more widely, interpreting Oodgeroo's highly visible career as a performative one in its entirety, both inside and outside the Australian film and media industries.

The final contribution, a selective checklist of Oodgeroo's writings by Janine Little, suggests the scope of her published and unpublished work (including uncollected oral material) which deserves in due course full exploration and documentation.

If education is the keynote of Oodgeroo's life, it is also the aim which underpins this volume. All those who have written pieces for this collection — all specially commissioned — were asked to demonstrate the ways in which Oodgeroo's legacy involves all aspects of human communication. Whether her message was spoken, printed, argued, drawn, broadcast, painted or performed, Oodgeroo was committed to a belief that questions always had to be asked — and she posed many pointed ones throughout her life. At the same time, she repeatedly offered suggestions, recommendations and solutions to all those who had the wisdom to listen. *Oodgeroo: A Tribute* is part of that process: while it is a tribute to the life of a remarkable woman it also aims, in its way, to continue the pattern of learning which Oodgeroo established throughout her career.

ADAM SHOEMAKER

NOTES

1 Jim Davidson, ''Interview: Kath Walker''. *Meanjin*, 36.4 (1977): 428.
2 Extracted from an unpublished article by Kristie Lorenz, with the permission of the author.

Reminiscence, Record, Travel

Growing Up with Our Sister Kath — Oodgeroo

Lucy Pettit

Kath was always a leader — she got us involved in all kinds of mischief. These are some examples.

Kath used to scribble from when she was young, when she wasn't writing she was exploring the mud flats looking for crab shells, quampees, oysters and anything we could eat. We followed her through mud and slosh with our buckets which we had made out of kerosene tins cut to size. My young sister, Vivian, had a black dog called Billy who went with us everywhere. He was devoted to our young sister. When she was a toddler she fell in the well and he dived in and held her up and barked to draw the attention of us and our mother. She was sitting astride him hanging on to the side of the well.

One day Kath encouraged our young sister Vivian to go with her. It was very quiet, only the dogs were barking — we had a little fox terrier by now. The girls were very quiet. Mum said to me, "Girlie, go see what the dogs are barking for." I found them. The dogs were digging a hole in the yard and Kath and Vivian said, "Look at that pretty thing down there." When I looked there was a big black snake with the reddest belly I ever saw. I raced back up to Mum and she grabbed her kettle of hot water and poured it down the hole and the snake was no more. I don't think the dogs were very happy. Mum looked at the girls and said, "See what that pretty thing was." It taught us quite a lesson.

It didn't stop Kath wandering. Next she took her younger sister exploring for flowers in the swamp. On the way back home along the beach they saw this beautiful shell; they picked it up and put it in the bucket, each taking a side of the handle. They were just about home when we heard them screaming. "What now?", says

Mum. ''Go and have a look girlie.'' When I got to them the side of the bucket was on the ground. ''What's up?'', I said, standing well away from the bucket; they said ''That shell has got a snake in it.'' When I looked a poor old tortoise was poking its head out for a breath of air. They took it home and filled up an old tub; he stayed for a while then moved back to the swamp.

The next time they went up the hill just above our place. They weren't gone long before they were back. Kath said, ''Look what we found Mum, a beautiful black ball; can we wash it?'' It stunk to high heaven. Mum said, ''You go take it back and let it go, it's an ant-eater and that is all it eats.''

All of us three sisters were fond of fishing and Dad decided he would fix up three leaky dinghies and we could have one each as we had our own fishing spots, but we had to take care of the boats, mend and paint them. Mine was white with blue inside. Vivian's was white with red. Dad made oars for us to row our boats when he said, ''Kath, what colour are you going to paint your boat?''. She sat thinking for a while then said, ''Have you got an old paint tin?''. Dad said, ''There is plenty of paint'', and she said, ''I'm going to see Uncle Fred'', so off she trots and comes back with a tin full of tar. ''I'm not going to paint all of mine. I'll paint the bottom and Uncle Fred said, the tar will last a long time.'' So Kath had a black boat that did last a long time. Kath said, ''I am going back to see Uncle Fred, he is throwing some nets away which we could wind around some rope and we can drag it up on the beach and catch some whiting and mullet.'' So all three of us went to see Uncle Fred — we soon had all the children wanting to help. We shared all we caught.

Whenever we wanted to fish in the blue hole we used to collect octopus to use for bait. Especially when the parrot fish were biting. We used to get up at dawn and go looking for mud crabs when the tide was right. When we returned home it was my place to work the engine; Kath's job was to jump aboard the dinghy which was anchored in the channel. Dad said, ''Now face the way we are going and when your sister slows the motor near the dinghy — jump!'' Kath did that but being left-handed she would turn around and always miss the dinghy and have to swim. She could swim like a fish.

Dad had a boat given to him. He decided to make a sailing boat out of it. He was pretty good at making sails and we helped him do the boat up. We used to sail up and down the channel at "One Mile". One day Kath wanted to go sailing and we were dressed in our shorts to go somewhere; anyway, we said we would just go for a sail up and down the channel; we were enjoying ourselves when the bung came out and the boat was filling up and Kath had her swimming togs on. We told her to jump out and tow us ashore. Kath got real stubborn for now and said no. My sister and I could see our clothes getting wet so I picked up the tiller and said "jump!", which Kath did when we got ashore. Mum who was watching us gave us the biggest lecture and grounded us. Needless to say Kath had the biggest grin on her face.

The next bright idea Kath got was to clean the creek. "Have you gone mad?" we said, "we want to play games." She got the pick and the shovel and Dad said, "What are you doing?" She said, "We are going to clean the creek." We boarded up all waiting where people used to come off the boats and enjoy the spring water, then Kath decided to take some of the bank away so we would have a swimming pool. It really turned out quite good and when the high tides came in we had a nice pool.

The wild parrots used to fly past our place in big groups and Mum used to say, "I would love to cook some parrots; I haven't had them for a long time." So we put our heads together and decided to put some wire on our sticks and hide behind a bush. When the parrots came over we would whistle and they would dive near us thinking there were hawks, so we acquired a roast dinner for Mum, but I couldn't do that now.

At the "One Mile" across the creek camped this dear old lady who we called Nana Watts. Her sons used to sail boats and were champions. She was a wonderful person. She used to collect all the children she could and bring them for holidays. If they wanted us to play they had to help us to do work and we did the same. We taught them how to swim and fish — it was wonderful. The most wonderful part was when she put on the first Christmas Tree. She had a present for every child in the "One Mile" and her and her daughters cooked and put on a beautiful party. She was the best white woman I ever met and I loved her dearly. The Watts family will always be remembered. That's when Kath was born: on Mrs Watts's son's wedding day.

A dear friend of mine and Kath's wrote the poem that follows. I think it is a lovely poem and I thank Eileen for writing it and hope you enjoy reading it. (Eileen's grandmother and Kath's grandmother were sisters.)

Tribute to Oodgeroo

She was a child of seven
When I met Oodgeroo
As children sat by bonfires
Sat upon the sandy shores
Where curlews wailed
When the tide was low
And tiny crustaceans
Made that clicking noise

The stars shone bright
The moon aglow
With perfume wafting off the sea
Sang songs and told our stories
And often played the fool
I've seen her put on boxing gloves
To settle a difference all in fun

Happy childhood days
On this beautiful isle
Enjoying all it had to give
While learning tribal ways
Memories come flooding back
Of this native child
Little did we know
The future ''chosen pathway''
The way for her to go

She wed and raised a family
And found the going tough
Two brothers prisoners of war
She joined the army
And played a part therein

She sought more education
But still she wanted more
Alone she went to distant foreign lands
Told them of our history
And of her people's plight
She plied her pen in literature
To further her just cause

Back home she fought so tirelessly
Debating far and wide
And lectured in the many schools
Where children sat rapt in awe
When told of our folklore

Visitors came from all around
And from the U.S.A.
I met them at Moongalba
In an open theatre
Set among the tall pine trees
And a campfire burning bright
We listened to her stories
And poems read by the campfire light

Laid to rest at Moongalba her beloved place
Tributes were paid to honour
Our one and only Ambassador
Her work is done in history — we'll remember
Rest in Dreamtime Oodgeroo.

Eileen O'Loughlin

Oodgeroo — An Inspiration for Members of the Darug Community

Pat Jarvis, Fay Richards and Edna Watson

A message stick sent to Oodgeroo of the Noonuccal from our brother Ken Upton of the Darug tribe, inviting her to visit Darug lands brought about our first meeting with Oodgeroo. From then on Oodgeroo became our friend and our sister.

Without Oodgeroo's continual encouragement we would never have had the courage to achieve what we have today. She taught us patience and a new-found pride in ourselves and our people.

Her favourite phrase "Don't Hate — Educate" will be a motto which we will try very hard to live by out of respect for our sister.

Oodgeroo took the Darug people under her wing and taught us skills that had been lost to our people. She was a person in high demand from people from all walks of life, but always she found time for the Darug.

When death came to our family the comfort Oodgeroo gave us came from the heart and made our loss easier.

She is a woman the likes of which this earth will never see again. She is sadly missed but walks with us every day.

A Mate in Publishing

John Collins

> And you and I are bought and sold
> Our songs and stories too
> Though quoted low in a falling market
> (publishers shake their heads at poets)
> Judith Wright, "Two Dreamtimes"

Australia in 1972 was almost ready for the "It's Time" election when I took a job at Brian Clouston's Jacaranda Press. Two years before, Kath Walker's *My People* had been published and, in spite of Judith Wright's all too accurate comment on publishers in her poem "Two Dreamtimes", which was dedicated to Kath Walker, the collection was already well into reprint.

Kath had established her sitting-down place, Moongalba, on North Stradbroke Island and had celebrated her return to something approximating normality after the turmoil of the sixties by writing some simple stories. These were stories of her childhood on Stradbroke and stories of the Dreamtime and they were written at Judith Wright's home at Tamborine. Twenty-one years later the collection is still in print and in two editions — one a paperback and the other a large cased edition illustrated by Aboriginal artist Bronwyn Bancroft. Does this mean we can still only cope with the happy and the pleasant but not the fire of her poetry?

At Jacaranda, after we celebrated the arrival of Whitlam and survived the 1974 Brisbane flood, Kath was known more by the mail her poetry generated than by her writing activity. For her, the seventies began as a decade of hope after the trials of the sixties. The fight for basic civil rights had been exhausting and in spite of the fact of the positive vote at the 1967 referendum (when Aborigines were at last officially allowed to exist and, more, be counted!), none of the badly needed reforms had eventuated.

Kath had played a significant role not just in the campaign focussed on constitutional change at the Federal level but as early as 1961 she had been State Secretary of the Federal Council for the Advancement of Aborigines and Torres Strait Islanders — or FCAATSI, as it came to be called — and for the whole decade was involved in the Queensland Aboriginal Advancement League.

Why had she become such a central figure? Probably, if we were to leave aside a great number of personality attributes, it was because she was the first person of Aboriginal descent to use language as a weapon. She had become the spearhead of the Aboriginal Movement as, with Faith Bandler and others, she traipsed the length and breadth of the continent campaigning, writing and speaking. Harold Holt, still quaking in the shadow of Menzies, would see no one but Walker when the delegation finally arrived in Canberra. After explaining carefully that he could do nothing without the support of all parties his first question to Kath underlined his status as a fifties politician, ''Is it correct that there are Communists in your organisation?'' Kath was quick to point out that all parties were represented but that the Association belonged to none of them. However, it is as well to remember that one of the reasons for Kath's linguistic, political and strategic skills was that she had learned a great deal from her Communist comrades of the fifties.

This beguilingly small person, who was by 1974 larger than lifesize, often brutally frank, as lively as quicksilver and teller of a thousand stories, readily acknowledged her debt to the one political party that didn't have White Australia as a policy plank, the Communist Party of Australia (CPA).

1950 had seen the sharpening of the Cold War and with it Australia's McCarthyite period. In 1951, Federal legislation banning the CPA had been declared invalid by the High Court and the Menzies Referendum was defeated. In the same year Frank Hardy had also won acquittal on a charge of criminal libel. However, the Petrov defection and the Royal Commission on Espionage were to follow and by March 1955 the Democratic Labor Party had come into being and Liberal Country Party rule was set fair for another decade.

On the surface, middle Australia was quiet and content and keen to re-establish itself after the war. But within the union movement the Groupers fought the Communists for control while those on the lower social scales received little comfort at all. The security forces (whether ASIO or other bodies) had an obsession with Communism and there was no more closely watched target than the associations of writers and artists. Dissident writers, those deemed to be purveyors of left wing thought, were dangers to the body politic. Fiona Capp in *Writers Defiled* comments:

> Overall the written word was considered more "insidious", "deadly" and "lasting" than soapbox rhetoric. The written word was more subtle — it could disguise its political intentions. (41)

Almost, as a matter of course, any group of writers — whether it was the Fellowship of Australian Writers, the Australasian Book Society or the Realist Writers' Group — came under immediate suspicion. Frank Hardy was one of the founders of the Realist Writers' Group which had amongst its members Judah Waten, Stephen Murray-Smith, Alan Marshall and John Morrison (most of whom were members of the CPA at that time). In 1954 a Brisbane branch of the group was formed for the advancement of local members.

Kath, at this time, was now a lone parent with two young sons — Denis was 10 and Vivian was 3. She had completed a Repatriation Course (shorthand and typing or the "dimwit" course as she liked to called it), had already joined the party with husband Bruce and via this membership was introduced to the Realist Writers' Group. Ian Syson describes the movement:

> [it] represented a forum for the discussion and production of working class literature. It was based on principles of collective criticism from established authors . . . and lesser well known members . . . working class people were presented with stories and poems that tried to link in with their own lives but they were also introduced to literary-theoretical issues that came from [*The Realist Writer*'s] regular articles on topics such as Modernism, Symbolism and the Australian Tradition. (71)

Kath had already started to write and people like James Devaney encouraged her to continue. The 1959 Brisbane program, which can be seen in *Overland*, shows that Kath was able (other

circumstances permitting!) to attend meetings on alternate
Wednesday evenings. There would be eight manuscript nights,
three readers' nights and lectures on the short stories of Lawson,
Vance Palmer and Gavin Casey and on the novels of Asia, France
and Queensland with David Forrest, the first winner of the Dame
Mary Gilmore Novel Competition, in the chair!

By 1959, however, there had been significant change in the CPA.
Hungary had been invaded and Stalinism had been denounced by
Nikita Krushchev. *The Realist Writer* had emerged as *Overland*
with Stephen Murray-Smith as editor.

Murray-Smith left the Party in 1958 but *Overland* remained
under ASIO scrutiny. This did not limit Murray-Smith's activity.
He travelled widely attending Writers' meetings. He was aware of
Kath Walker's collection of poems and one evening after a Group
meeting in Brisbane took Kath to a party at the Cloustons. He
introduced Kath to Brian and recommended publication. Brian,
in turn, passed the manuscript to his poetry reader, Judith Wright,
who gave the collection a positive report. Jacaranda obtained
support from the Commonwealth Literary Fund and, with a
foreword by the chief encourager, James Devaney, the all
important first volume of poems appeared in book form in 1964.
A real weapon had been forged. The original manuscript of *We
Are Going*, under its first title, "All One Race", was found in
the "unofficial" archives by longtime staff member Doug Pengelly
and the then Senior Editor, Col Cunnington, presented it to Kath
on the occasion of Channel Seven's "This is your Life" program
in 1979.

In 1962 Kath was in Adelaide for the Fifth Annual Council
Meeting of FCAATSI. With Aboriginal Elders as protection she
read her Aboriginal Charter of Rights which was the lead poem
in her first collection:

> Give us Christ, not crucifixion.
> Though baptized and blessed and Bibled
> We are still tabooed and libelled.
> You devout Salvation sellers
> Make us neighbours, not fringe dwellers;
> Make us mates, not poor relations. (9)

But mate she had become. For me it was a by phone, letter and
cheque relationship as the appeals multiplied for the use of her

verse. Most enquirers wanted free use because "their cause was just". Some wanted to use but alter parts to suit their own purposes; just a changed word here and there with no thought whatsoever about property rights! The beginnings of public demand on her words and her person had started in earnest.

In her second volume of poems, *The Dawn Is at Hand*, Kath wrote in the foreword:

> the criticism seemed to be that some of the poems were somewhat angry, bitter; as though even atrocities were never mentioned by nice people
>> *But hush, you mustn't say so*
>> *Bad taste or something.*
> And of course there was the malicious whisper of "Communist" (quite untrue) which now in Australia, as in the land of Joe McCarthy is automatically the answer to every vigorous protest against social injustice.

There were other malicious whispers too: "She wasn't a full black so it was the white blood that was writing"; "someone else has ghosted the work if not written it". The last accusation was made against Nellie Stewart who was supposed to have written parts of Hardy's *Power without Glory*, and against Betty Collins's, *Copper Crucible*. People did not understand (or did not want to understand) the methodology of the Realist Writers. This doubt as to genesis hurt Kath at the time and the hurt remained with her for most of her life. However, that did not stop her from her perceptive criticisms of the "comfortable" in the second edition of *My People*:

> Australian people are frightened by those who care deeply about something. They get embarrassed in public if people bring up uncomfortable subjects. They ridicule the earnest and those with convictions. This is reflected in their attitude to Government. It must be seen as strong and decisive, not too carried away with ideas like rights and freedoms and liberties although it is all right to talk dispassionately about "progress" and "enterprise". (42)

By 1965, *We Are Going* had been released in USA and Canada and, in 1966, *The Dawn Is at Hand* won the Jessie Litchfield Award. Other awards were to follow in 1966 — the Fellowship of Australian Writers Award and the Dame Mary Gilmore Medal.

The weapon was now very visible indeed and it was hardly surprising that in 1969 she was invited to be the Australian delegate to the World Council of Churches Conference on Racism in London. The period of overseas journeyings had begun.

Her wanderings during the seventies were extraordinary, and our mateship by phone and letter (mainly by phone because she was no great letter writer) was accentuated. Kath was in Malaysia, Papua New Guinea and Ghana as conference delegate (surviving a plane hijack on her return flight from Lagos) and she spent time as writer-in-residence at Bloomsburg State College in Pennsylvania. In between times she was at Moongalba busily entertaining and educating (with Kath there was very little difference); she made the film *Shadow Sister* with Judith Wright and became the Chairman (before political correctness!) of the Stradbroke Land Council.

At the end of this decade, which had begun with such hope but finished with deep disillusion, she gave a paper at the Australian National University entitled "Black Australia in the Seventies". It was included in the second edition of *My People*:

> I would say that the seventies were a watershed in Aboriginal history. When the decade started there was optimism and hope in the face of dreadful problems. Despite a good start, the optimism has gone, the hopes have been dashed. Only the dreadful problems remain. My people face dispossession and death despite the efforts of Aborigines and our white friends like Judith Wright, Nugget Coombs and Archie Kalokerinos, our future is grim...: However we do not react with despair and resignation. Perhaps I am still the incurable optimist of the sixties or perhaps I take a lesson from another poet who said, "Rage, Rage against the dying of the light...." (47-48)

So to the eighties, to the increasingly strident demands for land rights for Aborigines, the Bicentennial, Brisbane's World Expo and the emergence of Oodgeroo of the tribe Noonuccal.

In 1980, Kath Walker the environmentalist, tired of public speeches and protests, particularly against the sandminers and developers, decided once again to use print as a weapon. The wastage of Stradbroke — the Land of the Minjerriba — was very much in her mind as she put together a story for her grandchildren in particular but really for all children. As she discussed her plans, as colleague, with the Jacaranda staff it became very evident that illustrations were essential if it were to become a children's book.

In her little private time at Moongalba Kath had begun to sketch and paint. Just as the text for the story combined the Aboriginal view of creation with the all too modern era of destruction, so her sketches were a similar fusion of old and new. The only problem was the medium. This was solved when the Jacaranda Art Department found a decently spare box of felt-tipped pens. So, a unique style emerged which was not only to illustrate *Father Sky and Mother Earth* but which was to result in her first exhibition the following year.

Early in 1981, the Publishers' Association of China planned to make its first visit to Australia. Three years previously had seen the first visit of Australian publishers to China and the group had extended an invitation for a return visit by the Chinese. Sandra Forbes, then the Director of the Australian Book Publishers' Association, rang Jacaranda with the news that the Chinese, although pleased with their general itinerary, were disappointed by the absence of two elements: there was no editor on the list and there was no Aborigine.

As *Father Sky and Mother Earth* was at page proof stage I suggested that Brisbane should be on the itinerary and that I would ask Kath to do yet another barge trip from the island. With the Chinese dutifully suited and seated in the Boardroom of Jacaranda Press on 3 April 1981, Kath began her history of Australia with the words, "When the first white invaders arrived...", and from that point held her listeners spellbound (and the interpreters extremely busy) as she told the unvarnished story of white settlement. Mr Xu Liyi, the head of the delegation, was to remember the occasion with great clarity when five years later he was to listen to a proposal for a joint publication of Kath's China poems (see below).

That same year *Father Sky and Mother Earth* was launched at Warana Writers' Week and a number of reprintings followed. A paperback edition was issued in 1985 and a special edition of the work as part of a language program was released in 1990 with Oodgeroo as author.

But bigger issues were on the horizon. 1982 was the year of Commonwealth Games in Brisbane and it was a natural occasion for Aborigines and their supporters to highlight their demand for land rights. While competitors won and lost in the QEII Stadium Kath was one of the leaders in the Rights March through Brisbane. There was optimism abroad and it was reflected in the evening's television. Once again, a decade had opened with hope.

Kath, the activist, seemed to have found a new energy for things political and, at the 1983 Federal Election, stood as a candidate for the Democrats. She was unsuccessful but hopes remained high as Labor won with promises which included the granting of Aboriginal land rights. Many were the discussions during 1984, discussions which were more about politics than publishing and particularly about the growing strength of Labor's right wing. Kath was by turns raging and forgiving. Stradbroke had remained unbridged but the wider issues remained unresolved. The fact of Johannes Bjelke-Petersen as Premier and the seeming hopelessness of all opposition to his decrees only served to entrench Kath's desperate disappointment when the Federal Labor Government reneged on its land rights promise.

But during 1984 Kath was again overseas. This time she was a member of the Australia-China Council Cultural Delegation to China. The party was led by Caroline Turner (then Launitz-Schurer) and included Manning Clark, another of those "subversives" that had suffered from security's drive against Communism in the fifties (and whose reputation is once again under fire from the far Right in the nineties!).

The party travelled widely, but more importantly for Kath, the place and the people got her writing poetry again after a gap of over fifteen years. She returned to Australia, like many a soul who has been to China, excited, lively and renewed and it wasn't long before there was my mate in the office talking about publishing possibilities. My mind went back to our mutual friend, Mr Xu Liyi. In Beijing some little time later I met with Mr Xu and his colleagues and we explored the possibility of a co-publishing venture. Xu was a specialist in 12th century Chinese poetry. That and his memory of a day in Brisbane when he had heard of the "imperialist colonisers" clinched the issue.

So, the collection of poems, with a foreword by Manning Clark, and enlarged with the addition of a number of Kath's legends, was edited in Brisbane and typeset, printed and bound in Beijing. Its title, *Kath Walker in China*. It was something of an exercise in patience because although the agreement was signed early in 1987, the books didn't arrive in Brisbane until late in 1989. Kath quite rightly protested about the book's release when the news of Tiananmen Square broke. At first she refused to let the volume be released and wanted it pulped. However, by this time her son Vivian, after spending years in the States and in Sydney, was becoming more and more his mother's adviser, confidant and critic. He argued for publication but it was only after a new jacket had been designed that Kath relented and then only because she had taken up a suggestion to write a Requiem which was printed on the back of the jacket.

> Sitting in their comfortable
> Parliaments
> All these men
> Derive new ways,
> To uphold ignorance,
> To keep slavery alive.

Vivian had made sure, with good Realist Writer co-operativeness, that the poem, while specific in its target, carried a general message. So, on 5 April 1990, almost nine years to the day after the meeting with Chinese publishers in Brisbane, Kath's last book of poems with Oodgeroo as author was launched at the Chinese Club in the Valley by someone who in earlier days had been a visitor to Moongalba and a worker with Aboriginal Legal Aid, the new Labor Premier of Queensland, Wayne Goss.

In the mid-eighties Kath had been involved as both script adviser and actor in Bruce Beresford's film of Nene Gare's novel *The Fringe Dwellers* and with the encouragement of Ulli and Georgina Beier had held her first Sydney exhibition of paintings. Thus her almost last private world had gone public. It had been Ulli Beier who had invited Kath to be guest lecturer at the University of the South Pacific back in 1972. The exhibition became a book: *Quandamooka: The Art of Kath Walker* with Beier writing a perceptive and arresting foreword.

Then, one Saturday lunchtime, Kath was on the phone.

> "I'm ringing you from the Post Office at Dunwich."
> "Why?"
> "I've just collected a yard of telex. It's the longest I've ever seen."
> "Where is it from?"

"Moscow."
"Who signed it?"
"A fella called Gorbachev!"

Thus she announced her invitation to the International Forum for a Nuclear Free World for the Survival of Humanity. The forum was held in Moscow and Kath duly attended and gave readings of her poems. Her photograph, along with that of Yoko Ono, appeared in *Pravda*. So the ex-member of the CPA (and with Rodney Hall one of the better known graduates of Brisbane's Realist Writers) had finally made it into the halls of Communist USSR at the time of *Glasnost*. At least, the Berlin Wall was still standing!

On the way home from Moscow Kath stopped over in New Delhi and spoke on "Aboriginal Grass Roots Culture", a topic which was occupying an increasingly prominent place in her public speaking.

But there was now no joy in the political situation in Australia. The Land Rights campaign had stalled. All doors seemed shut fast. At this time, as on so many other occasions with all lines of advance seemingly blocked, Kath did what she had done many times in the past. She simply changed tack to get a fresh breeze. On this occasion it was a decision to discard the label of the white colonial past. Kath became Oodgeroo of the tribe Noonuccal, Custodian of the land Minjerriba, and Vivian took on his totem, Kabul, the Carpet Snake. The reaction from white Australia was mixed. A few understood but most, even among literary circles (the comfort zone sector), saw it as little more than a pointless gesture. Neither reaction bothered Oodgeroo. People were still anxious to use her work for the lowest fee possible whatever the name. What is more, the embarrassment caused by mispronunciation and misspelling only served to emphasise the ignorance of the Anglo-Celtic-European majority.

Then in 1987 came another phone call, this time from Moongalba.

"Will you come with me to Government House?"
"Whatever for?"
"To hand back that medal...."

We journeyed up Fernberg Road and crunched our way across the gravel of the Vice-Regal establishment. The Governor's Secretary met us and over a very polite but also very understanding cup of coffee the M.B.E. (awarded seventeen years earlier) was handed over. As we drove away Kath said: "I don't know whether it will make much difference but I certainly feel better."

Oodgeroo and Kabul had decided that Brisbane's World Expo was not just to be a celebration of white settlement no matter how many a politician talked of it as such. Together they produced the script and directed the production for the Rainbow Serpent Theatre — a mini son-et-lumière which attracted thousands during the Expo period. Many Aborigines and Aboriginal groups accused them of a sell-out, of pandering to the white establishment, but they stood firm. During the extended period of preparation and performance Oodgeroo lived in Brisbane with the cast and crew and telephone calls were replaced by many meetings.

At the age of 68, the pressure on Oodgeroo was great but she never faltered. In private, her doubts emerged. Her annoyance with her double identity and with the criticism and sometimes abuse that descended from all sides welled to the surface. She relived the fifties when her boys were "growing up behind her back". Yet she survived even confrontation of a quite violent kind.

One example of such an incident was when it was discovered that some of her drawings (those lost private things) were used by the Expo organisation on a promotional pamphlet, quite without permission or due acknowledgement. Oodgeroo and I met with the Executive Director of Expo (the former State Treasurer) to claim rightful compensation. The meeting began warmly (Oodgeroo said later that it felt like Mission stuff!) but ended abruptly and with many a harsh word and a firm refusal to acknowledge let alone pay reparations. Only after protracted proceedings negotiated via other parties were we able to secure the rightful dues. All this when Oodgeroo was a leading contributor to Expo's outstanding success.

Earlier in the year Oodgeroo received her first university recognition — an Honorary Doctor of Letters from Macquarie University. On the same day a similar honour was bestowed on Professor Arthur Delbridge who had piloted the Macquarie Dictionary through difficult times, by the Chancellor, Mr Justice Michael Kirby. Jacaranda Press thus shared in a unique double.

Oodgeroo's speech of reply was short and firm but polite: "This is a bit new for me but I suppose if I'm given an opportunity to speak again I ought to say more." When her chance did come she did!

Malcolm Williamson, the Australian-born Master of the Queen's Music, visited Australia in 1988 and after being introduced to Oodgeroo's poetry decided to get to Moongalba to meet her. In his foreword to a UK edition of her poems *The Dawn Is at Hand*, published by Marion Boyars, he described

> the mercurial personality of a poet who could recite poems, mostly not her own but which she admired, interposed with bawdy anecdotes, mercilessly accurate denunciations of those who deserved them and unstinted selfless praise of such colleagues as Manning Clark and Judith Wright.... (13)

Her ways had entranced but also sobered him as he said:

> Woe betide anybody impudent enough to open battle with that sharp intellect and flashing tongue as I know to my personal cost. Although neither of us knew it we were both in Moscow at the time of Glasnost:
>
> Kath: "Why didn't you come to hear me read?"
> Me: "I was at the Soviet Composers' Union."
> Kath: "Well, that was your bad luck, wasn't it?" (15)

Williamson produced his choral symphony *The Dawn Is at Hand* based on Oodgeroo's own selection and sequence of her poems and it had its premiere in the Brisbane Concert Hall. The Queensland Symphony Orchestra, soloists and the Queensland State and Municipal Choir performed to a packed house in late 1989. Once again there was applause, lots of it, but little remuneration. Williamson certainly was the driving force behind the UK edition of her poems and he did make valiant efforts to get the Open University to award Oodgeroo an honorary degree but he certainly got his own personal mileage out of the association. A prolific letter writer (when the spell is upon him), he did write to say that:

> Sir William Heseltine has informed me of Her Majesty's displeasure that Dr Oodgeroo, whom she especially wished to greet in Brisbane was kept out of the Presentation Room (at Expo). Those responsible have been invited to explain themselves, which in Royal Parlance, is very strong language.

Oodgeroo receives an honorary doctorate from Queensland University of Technology, presented by Deputy Chancellor J.J.W. Siganto, 24 September 1992. (Photograph by: Chris Marr)

Oodgeroo and I often wondered whether those loyal servants (worried about the return of the M.B.E. or perhaps worried about other things!) ever received a Royal reprimand.

Griffith was the second university to honour Oodgeroo. Kabul and his mother jointly wrote the speech in reply. Here was a platform and it was not going to be wasted. The substance particularly decried the fact that in so-called multicultural Australia

> Aboriginal people find themselves once again at the bottom of the socio-economic scale...We continually find ourselves firmly lacking any position or priority on any "ethnic" shopping list.... (*My People*, 3rd ed. 104)

They made a plea for Australia to let go of England and used Judith Wright's poem "Two Dreamtimes" to point to the divide that exists between conqueror and persecuted. Even more importantly they underlined their own ambivalence, their divided loyalties and the problem of achievement in a white man's world:

> There are many Aboriginal people in Australia leading [a] double existence who are irreparably damaged by the static they receive from their own families and communities for their achievements in the Anglo-Saxon world. Their strivings are seen as betrayal. (105)

Less than two years later Kabul had died of AIDS. This supremely talented artist and dancer had been with Denis, the activist elder son, one part of Oodgeroo's own ambivalence. Just as Denis had, via his sixties adoption of the Black Panther Movement, represented the violent longings of Aboriginal people, so Kabul, the sensitive, artistic, creative achiever represented the peaceful side. His being so cruelly struck down was a blow to Oodgeroo that with little doubt cut short her own life.

Kabul was buried at Moongalba on 23 February 1991. Always the artist/producer, Oodgeroo had a video made of the funeral ceremony, a ceremony that was to be replicated, though perhaps with less dramatic flair, by her own on 20 September 1993. Even in this period of personal sadness and depression Oodgeroo retained her humour and piercing wit. She showed it on two more public occasions: when the third edition of *My People* was released and when a third university, Queensland University of Technology, honoured her with a doctorate. When she was interviewed by Peter Ross for the ABC Television program *A Life* at her sitting-down place she was calm, compassionate, warmly humorous and gently optimistic:

> Frustrated still
> They walk away,
> With knowing smile
> And gentle voice.
> Now...
> We hope...
> For you have taught us
> ...hope...there is. (81)

But it was not to be hope alone. Back in 1968 in her paper on integration and Queensland society she had concluded:

> While we sit here and write papers the Aborigine and Islander stagnates for want of some action, so let's get on with the job.... (42)

And get on with the job of educating she did. Right up until the end she was travelling to the University of New South Wales assisting with the preparation of educational kits for all Australians.

Sadly, even in her last year the tendency of the white community to assume and take for granted still applied. One day late in 1992 Oodgeroo just happened to see *One Woman's Song — the Life of Oodgeroo Noonuccal* advertised in the press by the Queensland Theatre Company as one of their forthcoming attractions. At Jacaranda, we had also seen the ad and wondered. A phone call followed and then began the long argument to convince the State Company that permission was required as was a proper contract. Both came to pass eventually and with Oodgeroo's considerable help, the show, though thin, was far from a failure.

It seems fitting that the final words on my mate Oodgeroo, poet, activist, essayist, painter, filmmaker, educator and, above all, optimist, should come from John McLaren, the present editor of *Overland*, the successor to *The Realist Writer*:

> Her poetry was awakened while she was still known as Kath Walker by pity and anger at the state of her people, and to the end of her life she remained a valiant fighter for their cause. It is a matter of shame for white Australians that at the time of her death we had still neither begun to pay the rent for the land taken from them that we enjoy, nor had given proper recognition either to their claims on the land or to the cost they have paid for our occupation of it. (82)

WORKS CITED

Advertisement for Brisbane Realist Writers' Group. *Overland* 14 (1959): 12.

Beier, Ulli, ed. *Quandamooka: The Art of Kath Walker*. Bathurst: Robert Brown & Associates in association with the Aboriginal Artists Agency, 1985.

Capp, Fiona. *Writers Defiled*. Ringwood: McPhee Gribble, 1993.

Collins, Betty. *The Copper Crucible*. Brisbane: Jacaranda, 1966.

Hardy, Frank. *Power without Glory*. Melbourne: Realist Printing and Publishing, 1950.

McLaren, John [Obituary]. *Overland* 133 (1993): 82.

Noonuccal, Oodgeroo (as Kath Walker). *Father Sky and Mother Earth*. Milton: Jacaranda, 1981.

_____ . *My People*. 1st ed. Milton: Jacaranda, 1970.

_____ . *My People*. 2nd ed. Milton: Jacaranda, 1981.

_____ . *Stradbroke Dreamtime*. Sydney: Angus & Robertson, 1972.

_____ . *The Dawn Is at Hand*. Brisbane: Jacaranda, 1966.

_____ . *The Dawn Is at Hand: Poems*. London: Marion Boyars, 1992.

_____ . *We Are Going*. Brisbane: Jacaranda, 1964.

_____ . *We Are Going*. New York: Citadel P, 1965.

_____ . *My People*. 3rd ed. Milton: Jacaranda, 1990.

_____ . *Stradbroke Dreamtime*. Sydney: Harper Collins/Angus & Robertson, 1992.

Syson, Ian. "Approaches to Working Class Literature." *Overland* 133 (1993): 62-73.

Maang: bagaan di
(A message for my elder sister)

Philip McLaren

I was a young, impressionable Aboriginal Australian when I first saw her; she was stating her view on television, cleverly honing her point with flashing white teeth which contrasted against her dark skin. What a wit! It was May 1964, the era of black and white television: The Beatles, Twiggy, a mini-skirted "Shrimp", assassinations, Viet Nam and a new generation of Aboriginal Australians who voiced their concerns with such articulate ferocity they forced the world to listen. "Kath Walker — Activist" the superimposed caption read at the bottom of the frame of the television screen; and her teeth flashed and her cutting wit entered our living rooms. She said her first book *We Are Going* allowed white "ostriches" to see the Aboriginal point of view.

Later, in 1969, after returning from four years overseas, I was taken aback by the forthright manner of this new kind of black Australian. I had lived for the most part in North America: while away, I had grown used to "pushy" blacks and "well-spoken" native Americans. In Australia it was a time of equality, a time of referendums won and of rectifying national wrongs. And the black, female activist kept popping up and her wit became sharper with practice: the media had found a most articulate Aboriginal proponent.

I was not surprised to learn she was a poet. Though she was initially reluctant in producing her works, her incredible talent has ensured her poetry volumes a place of honour in Australian literary history. But she was also a philosopher: she wrote with great insight about black assimilation with a clarity of concern and vision usually reserved for theologians, gurus and progressive western philosophers.

Thirty years after I first saw her televised smile and absorbed her wisdom and her wit, I met her. She was now known as Oodgeroo of the Tribe Noonuccal: she had taken an Aboriginal tribal name and totem.

I had reached a juncture in my life where suddenly and with some trepidation I had begun to write seriously. My first manuscript — a fictional work based on the European settlement of my family lands at Coonabarabran — went on to win the University of Queensland Press/David Unaipon Award for black Australian writers. Oodgeroo was one of three who adjudicated and announced the winner. A few months later I went to Brisbane to receive the prize which was presented by Oodgeroo herself.

Outside the Queensland Cultural Centre Auditorium, on the South Bank of the Brisbane River, I waited for the award ceremony to begin with Roslyn — my wife — and Sue Abbey — a Senior Editor with the University of Queensland Press. "Oodgeroo has really been singing the praises of your work," Sue said, "she wants to meet you, to talk with you, before you go on."

And then I saw her hurrying up the staircase to the mezzanine level where we were standing. She was dressed in a long, light Indian cotton printed dress and wore R.M. Williams boots. She carried herself with confidence and everyone turned as she walked by. She appeared comfortable and confident with her celebrity status.

She expertly placed a cigarette in a long stem holder and lit it as we spoke. We had instant rapport, speaking on a level reserved for longstanding friends. I remember I surprised myself by holding a permanent smile as she offered advice: "It is by bold trust in our storytelling abilities that we win our readers," she said. "Don't be scared to push your ideas, push them hard. You've got a lot of work to do yet." Then she remembered lines from my work — ". . . The police then pushed the gunyahs to the ground, dragged the huts together with a rope tied behind their horses and burnt them in a huge bonfire." She paused then said, "I know people who had that exact experience."

I took on a load of advice from her that day before she leaned forward and tightly grabbed both my arms. "We desperately need more writers," she said. "It is our turn to tell our stories and we need as many writers as we can muster. You have written a story which will reach a lot of people. It is important to us all for you to keep going. Promise me you'll keep going.'' Her face was twisted by the intensity of her feelings. ''Promise me!''

I gave my promise.

Thirty minutes later inside the auditorium she publicly declared her strong affirmation of my work and called me forward to receive my award. My whole body welled with pride. She smiled at me as I made my way to the stage and I was immediately put at ease. We spoke again briefly after the ceremony and, with unusually long eye contact, she said goodbye.

Almost exactly a year later I took a break from my third novel to make a sandwich. I switched the radio on; the news reader solemnly declared Oodgeroo of the Tribe Noonuccal — Kath Walker — had just died. The great poet, the flashing smile, the wit and the wisdom were gone forever. I struggled to swallow my food. ''Oh, shit,'' I said out loud, alone. ''Shit!''

Epilogue

That same afternoon I received a telephone call from Pittwater High School, my sixteen-year-old daughter's school. I was asked if I would address the school to commemorate the passing of Oodgeroo. Of course I accepted.

When I arrived at the school for the service I was shown to the teachers' room where I was surrounded by eager non-Aboriginal people wanting to know about Oodgeroo. One female teacher had a story to tell about a chance meeting with her and, too soon, it was time for me to address the assembled student body and teachers.

With great care, teachers and students had arranged an array of Aboriginal flags to be flown at half mast. The podium also was decorated with red, black and yellow colours. I never thought I would ever witness such a day in my lifetime — a day when a non-Aboriginal Australian community would be compelled to express its loss and respect for one of us.

Oodgeroo's passing was well reported by the media that day. Heart-felt tributes were expressed from all levels of society. I had feelings of pride and emptiness: proud for what Oodgeroo had unselfishly accomplished for our people; and empty because of the void created with her passing.

I looked forward to the planned Warana Writers' Festival which was to be held at Oodgeroo's homelands on North Stradbroke Island. It, of course, became a commemorative festival — a celebration of Oodgeroo and her work. As I listened to her poems being read and dedications being pledged at the festival it warmed me greatly. I was not sad, instead I was overcome with the joy of the occasion, of place, her place.

Now I realise and experience some of the obstacles Oodgeroo had to overcome before her work could be widely accepted. For an Aboriginal writer to emerge to prominence in our country is to confront and endure enormous pressures from those who believe they hold exclusive rights to the published pages. Once pricked, bleeding racists make bad bedfellows. We experience vindictive critics blinded by jealousy and prejudice who vent their scorn by attacking the new literate black. Some push for blacks to return to the obscurity so carefully created for them, lest someone read the uncomfortable truth. To these self-appointed custodians of literature there is nothing worse than a black who can express the black view; even worse, for it to become popular. But others in the vanguard of literature with no regard of skin colour read the words and are immediately filled with expectation and excitement. Presently, international doctorates are sought by academics — I have been interviewed by them — their theses are based on what they term the newest, most exciting emerging writers of English in the world today: Aboriginal Australians.

What I feel at the passing of my elder sister was best written for Edgar — the closing lines of *King Lear*:

> The weight of this sad time we must obey;
> Speak what we feel, not what we ought to say.
> The oldest hath borne most: we that are young
> Shall never see so much, nor live so long.

I have seen in the arts that grieving the loss of past masters never ceases. The loss to Aboriginal literature of our gifted, precious champion, Oodgeroo, will be felt by numerous future generations of Aboriginal Australians unlucky enough not to have met her. I count myself as privileged to be encouraged and inspired by her and her work.

Oodgeroo as Friend and Artist

Ulli Beier

I first came across Oodgeroo's writing in 1965. I was living in Nigeria at the time, where Australia hardly entered one's consciousness. The slim volume of poems *We Are Going* shocked me into an awareness of the plight of the Australian Aborigines. Kath Walker, as she was then called, was the first Aborigine I had ever heard of, and by some curious set of circumstances she also became the first Aborigine I was to meet in person a few years later.

In 1967 I had joined the staff of the University of Papua New Guinea. About that time Dr Coombs had been appointed Chairman of the Australia Council and he decided that he wanted to do something to promote Aboriginal arts. On a visit to Port Moresby he casually mentioned to Dr John Gunther, the Vice-Chancellor of the University, that he was looking for somebody who could write a report on the state of the arts amongst Aborigines and make recommendations to Government on steps that could or should be taken to promote them.

John Gunther recommended me, presumably on the strength of my Nigerian experience, and surprisingly Dr Coombs invited me to make a six weeks trip to Arnhem Land and write a report for him. Neither my longstanding experience of Nigeria nor my brief acquaintance with Papua New Guinea qualified me for this difficult task in any way, but perhaps Dr Coombs was looking for an outsider with no axes to grind; someone uninvolved in the political or cultural controversies of Australia. It was an invitation I could hardly refuse. I told Dr Coombs, however, that I wanted to meet urban Aborigines before going to Arnhem Land in order to get a more balanced picture.

I stopped off in Brisbane and drove straight to Oodgeroo's house from the airport. I met her in the midst of a stormy political meeting, so this first encounter was rather brief. She found time to talk to me, however, and I took to her at once. Her small, frail stature belied her fiery temperament and her intensely alert eyes left one in no doubt that she did not suffer fools gladly. I cannot remember what we talked about, but I remember her quick, precise responses, her wit and her political anger tempered with tolerance.

Talking to other Aborigines later I was aware of the fact that they all had a lot to say, but that they lacked a platform, and one of my recommendations to the Australia Council was that there should be a political-literary magazine for Aborigines in which they could argue their case. The result was *Identity*, but unfortunately it was a rather tame publication during the first few years and it was not until Jack Davis took over as editor that the magazine acquired some teeth.

Conditions in Arnhem Land were a shock to me: Aborigines were treated like wards of court with no say in their own affairs and the Welfare Department made it very clear to me that this was the Northern Territory and that whatever Dr Coombs or anybody else in the Commonwealth Government might think, no one was going to take any notice of them in Darwin. But that is another story.

Soon after I had handed in my report Dr Coombs created the Aboriginal Arts Board — a predominantly white body, but with some impressive Aboriginal members like Dick Roughsey, Margaret Valadian and Oodgeroo. I was appointed to the board myself and this gave me the opportunity to meet Oodgeroo four times a year — until I left New Guinea in March 1971. We fought several battles on the board together, but more important and more inspiring to me were the long nights we spent after the meetings, arguing and talking over bottles of red wine. I learned a great deal from her about Aboriginal culture and politics in those years.

In the early days the Board found it hard to encourage Aborigines to make use of the opportunities it offered. Many Aborigines hadn't even heard of it. Others didn't know how to work the system. Some were suspicious of it. The result was that all the applications we received came from white people who wanted to do something for Aborigines. Most of these were good projects, but it was hardly what we had been set up to support.

The first Aboriginal proposal came from Oodgeroo herself, but surprisingly it met with resistance from the Board. Oodgeroo wanted to revive one of the old bora rings in Queensland. It was an exciting idea: the ancient sacred site should be given a new function; it should serve as a meeting place where children — both black and white — could be taught Aboriginal lore and survival skills. She asked the Council to put pressure on the Queensland Government to hand back the land to an Aboriginal trust and she asked for funds from the Australia Council to provide facilities for housing the children. She had requested a fairly modest sum — I think it was $40,000 — but some board members argued that Aborigines lacked experience in carrying out such a big project. So they proposed that the money should be used instead to have a "feasibility study" carried out by Queensland University students. I argued that since this was the first proposal to come from the Aborigines themselves and since the idea appealed to everybody, we should take our courage in both hands and give the money to the Aboriginal trust. But, of course, I was outvoted and the money was given to the students instead.

I was angry at the time, but looking back on those days one has the satisfaction of realising how much Australia has changed during the past 25 years.

Between 1971 and 1974 I lost contact with Oodgeroo because I returned to Nigeria to run an Institute of African Studies at the University of Ife. Even in this different environment, however, I tried to keep up my interest in Aboriginal arts and with the help of a wonderfully imaginative and energetic Australian Ambassador, Pierre Hutton, I was able to bring exhibitions of bark paintings, films on Aborigines and even a didgeridoo player to Nigeria.

I did not, at the time, succeed in bringing Oodgeroo to Nigeria. But some years later I pleaded successfully with General Garba, the open-minded Nigerian foreign minister, that Australian Aborigines should be invited to FESTAC, the Black Arts Festival in Lagos in 1977. Oodgeroo was sent ahead with a small delegation for preliminary discussions with the Nigerian Government. On the return journey her plane was hijacked. She told the story in an interview which I published in *Aspect* 34 (1986). It is a sensitive autobiographical sketch, revealing her indomitable courage, her wit and her honesty. Faced with the prospect of death she looks back critically at her past life and gives herself "bad marks for tolerance".

Her experience of Nigeria during FESTAC was not a happy one. She found Lagos chaotic and the people aggressive and violent. To control the traffic chaos on the streets of Lagos, General Gowon had the police issued with whips and ordered them to punish disobedient drivers on the spot. At least one Nigerian policeman got the shock of his life when he attempted to hit the driver of an official FESTAC car — a tiny woman jumped out of the car and battered him with her fists: "You leave my driver alone!"

As soon as I returned to Papua New Guinea contact was renewed with Oodgeroo. We met at "Writers' Week" at the Adelaide Festival, where I chaired a panel consisting of Oodgeroo, Hone Tuwhare and Wole Soyinka — a truly powerful team!

I must confess here that I had always considered Oodgeroo a wonderful human being — a person of absolute integrity and courage, possessed of a great fighting spirit and human warmth — but I had reservations about her as a poet. She had a vital message for Australians of all colours and she conveyed it in such a way that for a decade or so she was seen by many as the conscience of Australia. But was this rhetoric or poetry? Did poetry have to do with language or with messages?

But when she read her poems one forgot such arguments. Not that she was a conventionally polished performer. On the contrary, her diction was not clear, her voice was not trained — but she packed her readings with such intense emotion that she moved many people to tears. No professional reader could have made such an impact. When she read her poems you forgot about style, rhythm, poetic devices. Her personality came across very strongly.

I was able to experience Oodgeroo as a reader on two further occasions: once when we invited her to read during a festival at the Institute of Papua New Guinea Studies and again when she came to read her Chinese poems in our house in Sydney. On each occasion she held complete sway over her audience.

In fifteen years of friendship with Oodgeroo I had never been aware that she was not only a writer and a civil rights fighter, but also a remarkable artist. I "discovered" her drawings by accident. In 1985 I was to edit a special issue of *Aspect* which was to deal with Aboriginal art and literature. I hoped to have an interview with Oodgeroo and flew up to Queensland from Sydney. I had just returned from Germany — so we hadn't seen each other for several years.

It was a happy reunion when I arrived on Stradbroke Island. As in the old Sydney days, we sat talking until late into the night over flagons of port, which was her favourite drink. We spent three days discussing art and politics and life, but somehow I couldn't bring myself to do the interview — it would have brought an artificial, almost "official" tone into our meeting. It was a wise decision: as our conversation rambled on without purpose or direction, she mentioned casually that whenever she found herself under great stress during her politically active days, she would return to Stradbroke Island to recoup her energies. To unwind she would sit and "doodle". She drew shells, worms, spiders, snakes and sea pipes — all kinds of little creatures she had observed playing in Moreton Bay during her early childhood.

When I asked her whether any of these drawings had survived, she dragged out a battered dusty carton from underneath her bed. It was filled with delicate drawings carried out in coloured inks on cheap paper. She treated her art work with little respect — she was one of the least "precious" artists (or writers for that matter) I have ever met. Quite clearly it had been the process of *making* the drawings that had mattered to her, rather than the finished product.

Sitting in Oodgeroo's battered old caravan and looking at these drawings I felt that I was entering a very private world. The drawings are tender and they reveal a rather private interpretation of the universe — a mixture of Aboriginal lore, modern environmentalism and her own very individual whims and moods. The little creatures of her early childhood are symbols to her of the universe at large, archetypal images that have to be approached with awe.

I suggested that the drawings ought to be made available to a wider audience and that there ought to be a book. We didn't take this any further at the time, but a couple of months later Oodgeroo came to Sydney with the drawings. We made a selection and she spoke her comments onto a tape. What were meant to be no more than captions became beautiful prose poems, some of her most

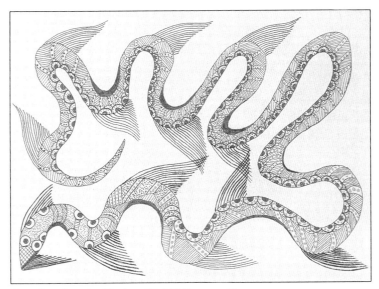

From *Quandamooka: The Art of Kath Walker*, page 24.

"The mother of life.

This is my interpretation of the rainbow snake.

I love drawing her, because my totem is the carpet snake, I draw a lot of snakes.

The rainbow serpent is very delicate and very strong and at the same time she is very beautiful.

I wanted to draw her with the beauty that she gives me; I wanted to bring out her beauty and her strength and her gracefulness.

Those wavy lines are not fins: I drew them to compliment the men in the Aboriginal world. They see the rainbow serpent as male, we see her as female. She is two things: male and female. I tried to express her femininity through the graceful, curling movement and the pretty pattern. Those delicate wavy lines are meant to give her a male look, without taking away from her femininity. I gave her something like a beard, I suppose.

In the dream time, the rainbow serpent lived under the earth, but nothing moved, they were all asleep.

Then the rainbow serpent broke through the crust of the earth and opened the way for all creatures. They came to the surface of the earth and lived."

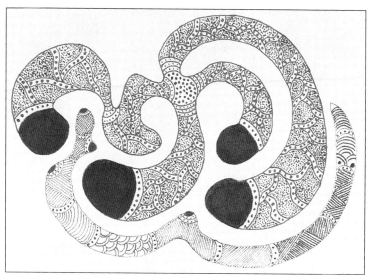

From *Quandamooka: The Art of Kath Walker*, page 36.

"This is my interpretation of earth worms.
People think, worms are ugly. But it's not true: worms are beautiful. They all cling to one another and intertwine and get themselves all mixed up.
When you separate them, you are amazed, how many worms there are!
You don't know, where one begins and another ends.
Earth worms always cluster.
All this curly movement!
Of course, it's the earth itself, that I am painting ultimately."

tender and delicate writing. The book *Quandamooka* was published by Robert Brown in conjunction with the Aboriginal Artists Agency. The book was launched in our home in Johnston Street, Annandale, on 15 November 1985. It was more of a celebration than a book launching. There was an exhibition of her original drawings which was opened by Bob Maza. Then Oodgeroo gave a reading of her Chinese poems, which she had written in 1984 when she was a member of an Australian cultural delegation to China. I think they are her most beautiful poems. In China she was far removed from the controversies and struggles of Australia. For the Chinese she was just another Australian, no one cared whether she was black or white. Oodgeroo saw China as a country that was tentatively trying to open itself to the rest of the world. She was sensitive to the cautious optimism of her hosts and trusted their goodwill. She was overwhelmed by the physical beauty of the country and by the hospitality of the people, and her visit was much too short to enable her to see some of the darker sides of Chinese life. Her heart went out to the Chinese people, her poems are full of anxious hope for them. They are more relaxed than anything she had ever written before: the political messages are still there, but they are delivered casually, almost offhand. The strange environment also allows her to see herself in a new light, and with a gentle touch she is debunking her own emotions as uncomprisingly as anybody else's.

On this occasion the reading was accompanied by Ernie Dingo (on didgeridoo) and Paul Adolphus (on harp and koto). Between them they created a beautifully integrated work of art. Unfortunately only a very poor amateur recording survives of the remarkable occasion. Oodgeroo enjoyed this performance immensely: "It will teach this young man that you can do something else with a didgeridoo than play rock on it," she said.

We ended up by paying homage to Oodgeroo. Our Nigerian friend, the musician and artist Muraina Oyelami, had just spent two months with us while working with me on his biography. We persuaded him to extend his stay for another week so he could be present at the exhibition. The night before the event we sat down together and searched our memories for ancient Yoruba praise poems and poetic formulas that might fit Oodgeroo's character, like "Kindness has never killed anybody, but it can give one a lot of headaches''. We compiled a little poem in her honour which I recited in English. Then Muraina chanted it in the original Yoruba language and finally, accompanied by Tunji Beier, he performed it on the Yoruba ''talking drum''. We ended with the lines:

> What can I eat to make me forget you —
> I shall never succeed.

While My Name Is Remembered . . .

Roberta Sykes

This is a personal account of my association with Oodgeroo
Noonuccal and the context in which it occurred.

A couple of generations of young Aboriginal people have now
been fortunate enough to grow up with, and share in the legacy
of, the works of Oodgeroo Noonuccal (Kath Walker). Most,
understandably, have no comprehension of what life was like
before this, and it's important for them in order to be able to
appreciate more fully Kath's work and times.

Although there had been an Aboriginal writer, David Unaipon,
whose work had been published before Kath's, he had not enjoyed
distribution or credit and, indeed, was virtually unknown until
almost forty years after his death.

When I was growing up in Townsville, North Queensland,
during the 1940-50s, there was really no Black literary figure of
any description for anyone of my generation to relate to. Our
world, and particularly the educational world — for those handful
of us who were given any access to literacy at all — was bereft
of our own imagery, history and aspirations. As children, we were
overwhelmed with the history, imagery and successes of white
people to the extent that we could not have been blamed for
doubting our own existence and worth and the existence and worth
of all, and any, other Black people.

While a teenager and young adult, a dribble of books with
Blacks on the covers began to appear and in my hunger to learn
of the experiences of people who looked like me, in the absence
of anything else, I read them. They were written by white, mostly
American, authors about slavery in the United States, in which
men, women and children of colour were sold as chattels, raped

at whim, and brutally butchered, maimed and murdered in an alarming variety of ways.

The world was a very hostile place for a young Black person, and even the other world — the world of the imagination — was polluted. Unfortunately, at this time — pre-Referendum, pre-citizenship, pre-anti-discrimination legislation — awful fantasy merely mirrored real life.

It was into this cold grey environment of hopelessness and despair that Kath struggled to step, to light a little fire, to take the chill off the air. But to have her work accepted, she had had to adopt a line that wasn't too threatening to the establishment. I didn't want to hear *We Are Going* (which she published in 1964), I wanted to hear how we were standing to fight.

Seven years later, when I was endeavouring to break through the wall into publishing with my own work, I found the marks she had left in the very same wall. Her blood and tears still stained the bricks and indicated where the wall was thickest, but also where again they could be made to crumble. How many Black writers now have scrambled through the little hole she made for us? Each one, though they still find it hard, must appreciate that their entry has been made easier by those who assailed the wall when it was strongest.

Kath and I skirted somewhat gingerly around each other for years, with very few opportunities presenting themselves for us to ever meet and talk. We attended state (Qld) and national meetings and, with hundreds present, the agendas were far more on our mind than personal matters, and so I saw her mainly across crowded rooms. I was impressed to see that a woman so diminutive in physical stature could bring a bustling and noisy room to an expectant dead standstill by merely appearing to be 'about to speak'.

On a few occasions she surprised me by approaching me — I would never have been game to approach her, such was her aura of privacy, reserve and power. Each time, she grasped my arm and said words to the effect of, ''I know what you're suffering. How are your children?'' Sometimes she said she knew what I was ''sacrificing''. Very few people saw me as a mother first, and framed their interest around my family. I was touched and at the same time shocked by the intimacy, and my answers were always brief.

From newspapers and grapevine I heard of Kath's adventures, China, Europe, Africa, and the struggles of establishing her dream at Moongalba. I dropped her a line from time to time, looking for ways to assist or for ways in which our organisations could cooperate. The network of women-initiated projects was, and remains, loose, but, in the main, they constitute a grid over this nation that is much stronger than, at first glance, they might appear.

During my study period at Harvard University (1979-1983), I wrote back to perhaps ten people for information at various times, Kath amongst them. She was one of the few who sent me over the information I sought, and she enclosed a nice handwritten card which read:

> Do what you've got to do, girl, and hurry home. I'm waiting for you.

It was a heartening message of warmth and solidarity, which I badly needed because I'd been feeling isolated and had begun to think that no one realised what it was I was trying to do. Kath's card conjured up for me her earlier confidences, that *she* knew of my suffering and sacrifice.

Because Kath lived at Stradbroke Island and I lived in Sydney, we continued to meet — after my return in December 1983 — only occasionally and in crowded venues, so the personal closeness we might have had never really had an opportunity to develop.

Still I kept tabs on her — her appearance in *The Fringe Dwellers*, for example, was almost a cameo of the Kath I knew, here one moment, gone the next, a notion which I shared with her — and from time to time we had a bit of a laugh about the way things were going in the movement. She kept tabs on me, too, evident from the comments she made when we paused to snatch a few words.

When the opportunity arose for me to write a book about Australian women high achievers, Kath (who had by that time rejected her name and embraced a traditional name of her Noonuccal people) was high on my list.[1] A niggling tiny voice in the back of my mind told me her clock was ticking over, and that if I was ever going to *know* Oodgeroo in her lifetime — over and above the public words in passing, the newspaper reports, grapevine information and opinions from others — I would have to get myself to Moongalba and let her share herself with me in her own setting, because Moongalba was the backdrop to the woman she was and the life she had led.

She rang me when I was in Brisbane and roused on me for not setting a firm date, which convinced me that she was as keen to spend time with me as I was with her. She had been ill and I had tried to work around meeting up with her in Brisbane, but this didn't work out. She gave me precise instructions of how I was to travel by train and ferry to North Stradbroke Island, and even which of the ferry companies I was to patronise because of an altercation she had had with one company. She would meet me.

The morning was blue and clear, but the wind was blowing hard and cold. Oodgeroo wanted me to interview her on the beach. The wind was so strong it was blowing the dry sand into a stinging frenzy which whipped our faces and clothing as I followed her. She didn't hesitate and knew exactly where she was taking me. Quite suddenly, and surprisingly, we entered a place that was no different from any of the other places we had passed to get there, but which was somehow an invisible cocoon against the wind. An area of a few square yards where the air was still, the sun shone warmly and the view of the water, wild birds and jumping fish, was incredibly tranquil and rejuvenating. Oodgeroo's smile told me she had wanted to demonstrate her absolute familiarity with every inch of her domain, and she was aware of how impressed I was.

Our conversation was wide-ranging. We covered her trips away, what she thought about Europe and other places she had travelled to, the details of how she felt when the plane she took — returning from Nigeria — was hijacked, and the empathy she experienced with the hijackers. Her moods rose and fell all day. She was angry at having been misquoted by the press, particularly after the hijacking, and her quiet voice conveyed her deep respect for the men who had died during the hijacking, and for the bravery of the pilot. Discussing this subject led her to other ''un-sung heroes'', and other times when the press had betrayed her.

She spoke of people whom she regarded as friends, and others whom she thought of as enemies and traitors to the movement, but who — because an Elder had, long ago, told her she must — she struggled to love despite their shortcomings.

I talked about the sterile white literary environment in which I had grown up and how I felt it had negated me. I wondered, since her exposure would have been similar, where and how she had found the courage to write and to make publishers sit up and take notice. She told me she had reached inside herself for material and nerve, and that she had continued to do so, and that, in the early days, a mere handful of friends had sustained and encouraged her. She blessed them.

After I had taped several hours, I told her that I would have to edit the interview down and that I would, as I did with everyone who appears in *Murawina*, send her the interview which she would be free to change. She said, "Don't worry about it. I trust you, so you can write anything you want." I asked her why she was so trusting, thinking of her earlier rages against people who had taken her words and twisted them. Oodgeroo replied that while she hadn't read everything I'd written, everything she had read had impressed her. I was humbled, and when she charged me with a responsibility to continue writing — "Write anything, just keep doing it" — I understood she was telling me she was going soon.

Our conversation somehow moved quite naturally from there to the subject of death. Underneath her occasional abrasiveness, she carried an awesome sadness about her life, and she had been wanting an opportunity to share her grief. It was a private sharing about her life which I understood was only for me. Then we began to talk about her death.

She told me her plans, where she intended to be buried, and how her spirit would hang about and in what forms. "Oodgeroo," I said, trying to approach the subject obliquely, "you know that when a person of your stature dies, it will be expected that we do not mention your name, probably for years, as a mark of respect." She knew I was thinking of the book I was working on, and the possibility that her prediction of her imminent death would perhaps mean I would have to leave her out of my book, or withdraw the book from circulation for many years.

She put her hand on my arm, her familiar gesture to draw us closer together, and chuckled. She said she admired my forthrightness, how I kept my eye on my goal. "When I die, I want people to shout my name. Write your book. All my life I've been teaching, teaching, and I'm going to keep right on teaching beyond the grave. Nothing I've ever written is to be withdrawn, no pictures of me to be turned to the wall. From beyond the grave I want to keep looking them in the eye. Remove nothing, change nothing, let me keep teaching from beyond the grave. Help me to keep teaching. While my name is remembered, I teach."

Mid-afternoon, and after her photo-session, Oodgeroo took me back to her house. Her dogs distressed me, she kept them for her own safety and they were chained. There were things she wanted to show me, bits of her lifestyle she wanted to familiarise me with. She showed me the separate dwelling she had installed for Vivian, and her own simple accommodations.

At day's end and when I'd convinced her I just couldn't "stay a few days", she loaded my bag with passionfruit and took me back to the ferry. On the way, we went by the old cemetery and she explained its history and significance. She stood by the pier and waved until I could no longer see her, and despite the spiritual and visual beauty of her paradise in the twilight evening, I knew our sharing was complete and I was heavy of heart.

By faxed messages and phone conversations, her interview for my book was edited to her satisfaction and, as she had said, she didn't request any changes and was happy with those parts of our talk that I had chosen to accompany her portrait. Oodgeroo didn't live long enough to see the publication of the book.

Oodgeroo's adult life was spent in quest of answers, and in her early days, she recalled, she was often more wrong than right in determining the direction she should take. There were few opportunities for a young Aboriginal girl in her day, but the ones she saw, she pursued.

Oodgeroo's legacy, which she has left for future generations, is vast. Moongalba, for example, is an idea that she created and fought for, to enable young people to get in touch with the land and with nature. Her lifestyle was simple and she was scrupulous about waste, especially of any living creature. She deplored vandalism and its effects on nature, but had a deep respect for the balance which interrelationships between animals and humans require. "The fowls and fish of the world feed me, and eventually I will be the food of the worms of the earth, and then the fowls and fish will eat the worms and our circle will be complete," she confided. I wasn't startled because she was just voicing something we both knew, so we laughed.

But Oodgeroo's main talent was her writing, her sharing of her struggle and her ideas. These she has left as gifts for all of us. Her poems, through their different stages, mirror her own development and growth, as much as they also provide for us a sort of barometer for what the public would, at various times, accept from her as a Black woman. She was canny about knowing how far she was going to be allowed to go, then drawing her bead right on that line and waiting until the line slackened a bit so she could push for a little bit more. Her advances laid down pathways for other Black writers whose duty it is to push the boundaries as far as they will stretch before they break and fall away. And when these artificial boundaries — which restrict the opportunities of Aboriginal people and cause ill-will between people who wish to live in harmony in this country, which is Oodgeroo's country — fall away under the pressure of people and time, let us hope that those who witness this great event remember to shout her name — OODGEROO — so that she can continue to teach.

NOTE

1 *Murawina: Australian Women of High Achievement.* Text by Roberta Sykes. Photographs by Sandy Edwards. Sydney: Doubleday, 1993.

Oodgeroo in China

Nicholas Jose

Oodgeroo, or Kath Walker, as she then was, visited China from 12 September to 3 October 1984 in a delegation comprising Caroline Turner (as leader), Eric Tan, Rob Adams and Manning Clark.[1] The delegation was organised by the Australia-China Council (ACC), under the auspices of the Department of Foreign Affairs, in response to an invitation from the Shanghai People's Association for Friendship with Foreign Countries, an arm of the Chinese Foreign Ministry. In the composition of the delegation, with its broadly cultural focus, one can perhaps see the hand of Geoffrey Blainey, the ACC's first Chairman, and then Executive Director Jocelyn Chey, who must have enjoyed advising the Shanghai authorities that Oodgeroo's "father was of Noonuccle Tribe, Carpet Snake totem". Caroline Turner, Deputy Director of the Queensland Art Gallery, was an ACC member, as was Perth surgeon Eric Tan. Rob Adams represented the Australia Council. Manning Clark had the distinction of having his *Short History of Australia* published in China in 1973, for internal distribution in government circles only, with the warning "the author is a bourgeois historian. Many of his opinions are not in line with Marxism."

The visit came at a rosy time in Australia-China relations. China's "economic reforms" and "open-door policy" were well underway and the devastating extremities of the Cultural Revolution were being firmly repudiated. From the Australian point of view, China had been identified as a regional and trading partner to be cultivated. The ACC, along with other Australian organisations, was implementing a vigorous program of activities designed to extend people-to-people as well as official ties. The

1984 cultural delegation was a highwater mark in this process, a happy and well-managed visit that pushed back the boundaries of what was possible and resulted in some enduring recommendations and initiatives. To look back after ten years is to discover, perhaps with surprise, the long-term effectiveness of cultural relations in enabling insights and contacts that can be built on in the future. Training exchanges for young people developed from the delegation's recommendations, for example, with medical students from the University of Western Australia spending part of their course in Chinese hospitals, and Australian students of Chinese language being placed in organisations in China for work experience. A vigorous sister relationship was established between Shanghai and Queensland, which has facilitated the exhibition of treasures from the Shanghai Museum in Australia, and Shanghai's representation in the first Asia-Pacific Triennial of contemporary art at the Queensland Art Gallery in 1993. There are many more such flow-on benefits.

Part of the agenda came from the Shanghai authorities who in 1984 were keen to establish in the minds of Australian administrators that a whole range of activities was possible with Shanghai, more or less independently of Peking's control. Thus a lasting message was sent about devolution (and rivalry) in China, as the monolith of centralised power fissured. Australia identified the need to develop polyvalent relationships with China. The delegation's visit took place in the wake of the shortlived, but chilling, Anti-Spiritual Pollution Campaign of 1983, a conservative backlash against liberalisation, pluralism and Westernisation in the ideological sphere, which set the critical parameters of how the Chinese Communist Party (CCP) would handle the consequences of social change and modernisation. The policy of Australian governments, then and now, has been to support liberalising and reforming elements in Chinese society, and the distinguished cultural delegation's visit in September-October 1984 can be seen against this wider diplomatic background. The delegation's official host, Mr Li Shoubao, then Vice-President of the Shanghai Friendship Association, among other functions, has proved over the years a highly effective servant of his government's interests. At the October 1st National Day banquet in Canton (Guangzhou), the delegation met Mayor Ye Xuanping (son of revolutionary Field Marshall Ye Jianying) and Provincial Party Secretary Xie Fei, both of whose reformist stars continued rising during the 1980s. Meanwhile in Australia Geoffrey Blainey's comments on Asian immigration were causing a local variant of an anti-spiritual pollution campaign and were "something of a catalyst", Caroline Turner recalls, for the travellers' sense of themselves as Australians while in China.

Their itinerary was mostly a standard one, combining historic and scenic sites with cultural visits: Peking and the Great Wall, Xian and the Entombed Warriors, Shanghai, Hangzhou, Guilin and a cruise down the Li River, and finally Canton (Guangzhou). Of the meetings arranged for the group, highlights included a lively seminar with staff and students of the Australian Studies Centre at Peking Foreign Studies University, under the guidance of senior literary scholar Professor Wang Zuoliang and Australian history specialist Professor Wu Zhenfu, whose husband Professor Hu Wenzhong, Director of the Centre, was visiting Australia at the time.

Manning Clark, who had undergone major surgery a year earlier, was thrilled to stand atop the Great Wall. Dr Tan advised him to take it easy. Manning's fear that he might have cancer (he didn't) heightened his experiences during the visit. He wrote later: "We were all very excited. We were all like human beings who had fallen in love at first sight."

In Xian the group visited Huxian, where the famous peasant painting movement began in the 1950s. They were fascinated by the lively work, with its blend of folk exuberance and contemporary socialist realism, and by the management of a movement that, with a modicum of intervention, allowed working people to give seemingly spontaneous expression to their lives in a form that could also succeed in the marketplace. During a meeting with the artists, Oodgeroo passed Rob Adams a Qantas postcard on which she had scrawled: "If you love me, you'll pinch that painting off the wall for me." There are parallels between the Chinese peasant painting movement, which by the 1970s was seen by some outsiders as a representative achievement of Maoist cultural policy, and the development of Aboriginal art in Australia from the 1970s. Perhaps at Huxian Oodgeroo saw in action some of the possibilities she was working towards in her own community cultural centre, Moongalba, at North Stradbroke Island.

Oodgeroo and Manning Clark, together with other members of the Australian delegation, atop the Great Wall of China, September 1984. From the left Li Shoubao (host), Caroline Turner, Oodgeroo, Manning Clark, Eric Tan. (Courtesy of Caroline Turner)

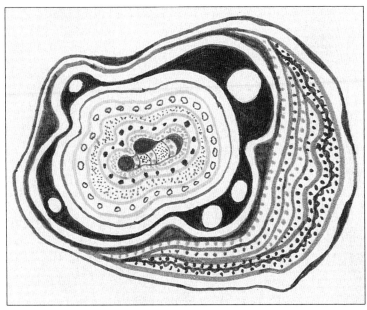

Oodgeroo's illustration of a pearl shell, sketched during her visit to China, and given to Caroline Turner (see page 48). (Courtesy of Caroline Turner)

In Xian Oodgeroo and Manning sang "Waltzing Matilda" to a group of Young Pioneers, the CCP's cubs and brownies. In Shanghai preparations for the National Day celebrations were underway when the group visited the Shanghai Municipal Children's Palace, and this time Oodgeroo talked to the children about Aboriginal art, while Manning danced with them. The group was in Canton when October 1st arrived and they watched on television the military parade through Tiananmen Square that marked the 35th anniversary of the founding of the People's Republic of China. It was the first such parade since 1959, and, according to an official spokesperson, "was not intended as a show of force, but as a display of defensive strength", boosting the morale of the People's Liberation Army, which was unhappy about aspects of the country's modernisation drive and now, under Communist Party leadership, was well on the way to becoming a sophisticated fighting force (*Far Eastern Economic Review* 11 October 1984: 16). There was another reason for celebrating, which would not have been lost on the citizens of Canton. The joint declaration between Britain and China confirming the return of Hong Kong to China in 1997 had been signed across the border in Hong Kong only a few days before, on 26 September 1984.

I can only speculate on how the members of the Australian cultural delegation responded to the momentous events going on around them, to their encounters with China, or to their sense of themselves as representatives of Australia, which they were invited to articulate at meeting after meeting. Accounts of the trip exude euphoria, perhaps not an unusual response for first-time China visitors (all except Tan), but enhanced here by the determined optimism of China in 1984 and by the personal chemistry of the group. Clark claimed it was the happiest such trip he was ever on. The delegation members developed friendships with each other that were to endure. In writing and conversation they convey a great sense of warmth towards each other and towards the China they experienced together. The central element in the group dynamic was the relationship between Oodgeroo and Manning. While she had tremendous respect for her old friend, Oodgeroo was not overawed by him. When Manning gave a panoramic picture of Australian history, Oodgeroo was not afraid to present a different version, emphasising the white man's invasion of the country and "blood in the streets". It amused the Chinese that one black woman would dare to differ from the great historian. A photo taken, of all places, at Chiang Kai-shek's villa, shows Oodgeroo cheekily resting her head on Manning's knee, as he looks sternly at the camera, in an ironic tableau. Oodgeroo saw herself as an ambassador for Aboriginal culture. At first she may have been overwhelmed by the impact of Chinese culture, acknowledging the contrast between its achievements and the fate of her own comparably ancient culture. She was homesick, and the tug of home led her to relate China always back to her own cultural heritage, which she had a tremendous capacity to share with the people she met. In this way Oodgeroo connected herself with China too.

Within the group, and within Oodgeroo herself, a momentous event of another kind was taking place. She had written no poetry for some six years before her trip to China. Her life was extraordinarily busy, activist and public. She had private problems to deal with. She had an established literary reputation. But for any writer, not to write, however easily explained, must be an uncomfortable condition. One morning Oodgeroo said to Manning: "I'm pregnant again." She meant she had started to write poetry. During her three weeks in China she produced a suite of sixteen poems. The first one, published as "China . . . Woman" was inspired, if I have reconstructed the circumstances correctly, by a tour of the Forbidden City ("in a word overwhelming" is how Caroline Turner reports it) in Peking on 17 September 1984 and written over the next few days. By 19 September the travellers had flown to Xian, which was where Rob Adams photographed Oodgeroo sitting on a step outside the Wild Goose Pagoda apparently writing the first poem of the series.

"China . . . Woman" is general and synoptic, giving voice to the affinities Oodgeroo found with China. As an Aborigine she compares the Great Wall to the Rainbow Serpent; as a woman she conceives China as dignified and fecund; as a revolutionary she registers the weight of the past, the struggle for change and also, in a sharp image of Beihai, the once-imperial park, some of the ironies of the present:

> High peaked mountains
> Stand out against the sky-line.

The great Wall
Twines itself
Around and over them,
Like my Rainbow Serpent,
Groaning her way,
Through ancient rocks ...
China, the woman
Stands tall,
Breasts heavy
With the milk of her labours,
Pregnant with expectation.

The people of China
Are now the custodians of palaces.
The wise old
Lotus plants,
Nod their heads
In agreement. (*Kath Walker in China*)

In their published form, in sequence, the poems offer a journal of the trip, and, as befits diary entries, they are informal, spontaneous, catching fleeting pictures and unresolved thoughts, tied to the specific evanescent occurrences of the visit. They are not without a sense of comedy at the situations in which the visitors find themselves:

Manning and I
Offered to sing
Waltzing Matilda for them.

I think they liked it,
Or, maybe, they were
Showing us,
How polite they can be.

Then, they sang a song for us.
A song of the young pioneers.
We liked it too
And before we left,
We cupped our hands, and called for them
Our
Australian coo-ee.

Elsewhere there is a sense of the irony of scale, as the travellers find their own personal connections with, or reactions to, what is laid before them.

> We are shown the pavilion,
> Where they caught
> Chiang Kai-shek.
> It's halfway up the mountain
> Of the black horse.

> Later ... I sketched a pearl shell
> and gave it to Caroline.

Impromptu and seemingly effortless, the poems enact an open, fluid, wry and insightful response to China, in straightforward terms, aware too of sadness on the other side of hope:

> We saw a giant panda
> At the zoo.
> He wasn't very happy,
> He was sick.

China hands say that if you go to China for a month you write a book, for six months maybe an article, but if you go for a year or more you will never write anything, as the ever-increasing complexity of your knowledge reduces you to silence. Short-term visitors are faced with a barrage of bewildering, often incomprehensible impressions, and under the pressure of journeying through a hugely different world, they struggle with exhilaration and exhaustion to formulate reactions. Oodgeroo's response, in her effusion of poetic fragments, sidesteps the need to reach conclusions, while registering with sensitivity the wonder (in every sense of the word) that she experienced. The underswell is the personal reference back to herself and what she knows. In the Reed Flute Cave at Guilin, for instance, she writes:

> I shall return home,
> And I'm glad I came.
> Tell me, My Rainbow Spirit
> Was there just one of you?
> Perhaps, now I have time to think,
> Perhaps, you are but one of many guardians
> Of earth's people ...

The China poems are less public, less oratorical than her more familiar work. In their free, spare, elliptical immediacy, they have an imitation-Chinese quality, reminiscent at times of Maoist revolutionary verse (for example, "Sunrise on Huampu River").

Oodgeroo may have been relieved to escape for a while from her public role back in Australia. She enjoyed herself in China. She took the toasts at banquets while others piked out, and Eric Tan and Rob Adams had the job of sourcing the liquor for after-hours. She let her creativity flow. The poem "Peasant Painters" she wrote on the plane from Xian to Shanghai. Throughout the trip she made pastel drawings, and after Eric Tan bought her Chinese brushes and inks she experimented with Chinese painting. She copied out her freshly composed poems and decorated them with snakes and other personal emblems and presented them to people she met. She was less impressed by great historic sites and occasions than by the direct experience of place, people and lived history, by walking round markets and countryside, for example, by meeting with students with whom she engaged as the sparkiest sort of teacher, and above all by children — partly because they took her back to her own grandson and the children who visited her at Stradbroke Island. As Caroline Turner recalls, Oodgeroo "grew in energy all the time throughout the visit ... She had a marvellous intuitive sense of place which came in part from a poet's sensitivity and in part out of her Aboriginality but also from her acute intelligence and ability to respond to people."

Oodgeroo was happy to go home, but she had come to China gladly. She remembered Chinese sailors who had come to Stradbroke Island and mixed peacefully with the Aborigines, suggesting ways of relating that existed outside the historical, geographical and cultural constructs established by Europeans. Chinese were trading sea slug from Australian tropical waters from the late seventeenth century, as Oodgeroo seems to know when, in touch with telling details, she writes a caption to her drawing of a Stradbroke Island sea slug:

> There are very many different types of sea slug. The sea slug that the Chinese people like to eat, is very very different; it's very hard and it hasn't got any pipes. It's what people call a sea cucumber. (*Quandamooka* 46)

She was also aware of the international communist role in opposing racism and oppression of indigenous peoples. An important memory of Kath Walker's youth was of the public stance taken by the Communist Party of Australia in exposing a racist incident in Queensland. China under Mao had styled itself the leader and advocate of developing peoples and the Third World. As far as I know, the first Aborigine to visit the People's Republic of China was Gary Foley in 1974, who brought back ideas about the people's communes, among other things (''An Aboriginal in the People's Republic of China'', *New Dawn* July-August 1974: 1-3).

By the 1980s, however, China's credentials in this regard were wearing thin, as relationships with the developed world took priority. In developing countries, China's emphasis shifted from aid to trade. China's treatment of her own minority peoples had come under scrutiny and it was known that practice fell far short of rhetoric. China's occupation of Tibet, in particular, was becoming a critical issue, even as the Chinese authorities in the middle 1980s appeared to back-pedal on their earlier genocidal policies. China's sensitivity on these issues led to the propaganda use of a ''pot calling the kettle black'' approach to other countries. In the case of Australia, the Chinese government focussed on the appalling plight of Australian Aboriginal peoples as part of a larger indictment of capitalism. There was a degree of hypocrisy in this concern. Chinese xenophobia can take particularly repellent forms in relation to black people, and even at its most benign it delights in the strangeness, the ''colour and movement'', of black cultures.

Many Chinese have shown an excited curiosity about Aboriginal culture, with an appreciation of its antiquity and distinctiveness, sometimes even recognising similarities with ancient Chinese culture, but at other times mainly savouring it for its perceived exotic and primitive qualities. Since 1984 different kinds of Aboriginal art have been exhibited in China, and have been well-received. There have been further Aboriginal delegation visits. One included Aboriginal photographers who were retracing the links between the Rainbow Serpent and the Great Wall.

It was into this complex environment in 1984 that Oodgeroo went and no doubt she saw it all for what it was. I don't imagine it changed the view expressed in the first poem of *My People*, ''All One Race'' (illustrated, incidentally, with a caricature of a pigtailed Chinaman):

Black tribe, yellow tribe, red, white or brown,
From where the sun jumps up to where it goes down ...
I'm for all humankind, not colour gibes;
I'm international, and never mind tribes.

But there were some awkward moments. The seminar at the Shanghai Foreign Languages Institute was less dynamic than the counterpart occasion in Peking. "The students and audience in Shanghai seemed confused by many of the things we said," comments the report. This may have been because the students were insufficiently informed about Australia. It may have been because of internal resistance at the Institute to the development of an Australian Studies Centre (it subsequently transferred to East China Normal University, Shanghai). Or it may have been because the imposing official Shanghainese presence intimidated the Chinese participants, causing open inquiry to become entangled with diplomatic facadism. The audience seems to have been uncomfortable about the delegation's frank criticism of aspects of Australia. In the wake of the Anti-Spiritual Pollution Campaign's repression of intellectuals, the audience must have hoped that the visiting intellectuals would identify Australia with pluralist and humanist values. Students may have been puzzled to hear Manning Clark speak of China as a beacon to Western intellectuals. Sinologist Dr Geremie Barmé was in the audience as an uninvited guest and recalls it as a distasteful occasion. Regulations were in force at the time to prevent "unattached foreigners" from mixing with the local populace. Barmé's independent presence in Shanghai, by contrast to the carefully managed presence of the delegation, meant that he came under secret police surveillance. It seemed to him that his fellow Australians were irresponsible not to consider how their remarks might be taken or used in the local context. He remembers feeling a sense of "national betrayal", that led him to question his sense of himself as an Australian who was nonetheless deeply committed to understanding China.

By the time the travellers reached Guilin, they were aware that there had been virtually no contact with China's so-called minority nationalities. In Guangxi Zhuang Autonomous Region, the area around Guilin, the "minorities" made up some 70% of the population. The group was joined by Roger Brown, Australian

Consul General in Shanghai, who, with Eric Tan, sought to rectify this omission in the program. Oodgeroo was interested, although it was not something she pushed for. In the event the delegation met some official representatives of the Zhuang people, but there was recognition by this late stage of the trip that the program had been filtered. ''We were keen to meet with minority people, and thanks to the admirable Mr Fu [of Shanghai Friendship Association] this was done. However, we felt our local hosts in Guilin could have arranged a one-day trip to visit the minority people considering the time we had available in Guilin,'' notes the report. The minorities in the field would probably not have presented as smartly as their official representatives.

Among the many results of the visit was a proposal to publish the poems that Oodgeroo had written during the trip in a bilingual edition, as a joint venture between Jacaranda Press and the International Culture Publishing Corporation of China. The proposal was brought to fruition by John Collins, thanks to his well-established contacts with Chinese publishers, notably Mr Xu Liyi, then Vice-President of the Chinese Publishers Association. The suite of China poems was published with additional material, including an enthusiastic foreword by Manning Clark and evocative photographs of the trip taken mainly by Rob Adams, in a volume dated 1988, *Kath Walker in China.* The Chinese translations by Gu Zixin are accurate, although inevitably with minor differences. The lines quoted above about the sick panda, for example, become: ''He wasn't very happy *because* he was sick.'' This slightly shifts the directness of Oodgeroo's sympathy for the (highly symbolic) giant panda's plight.

The volume is unique in many ways. As far as I can establish, it contains the first Aboriginal writing published in China. It is the first single volume of an Australian poet's work, male or female, published in China, and the first joint literary publication, and so on. Some 2000 copies were taken for distribution in China, the remaining 850-1000 were sent to Australia. They arrived in Brisbane not long after the Tiananmen Square massacre of 3-4 June 1989. Witnessing Tiananmen Square at a happier time, Oodgeroo had written on 18 September 1984:

The big square
Welcomes

Her sons and daughters . . .

The tragic, and potentially embarrassing, irony of these lines would not be lost on Australians. A new dustjacket was printed incorporating on the back cover a new poem, "Requiem", condemning the male politicians everywhere who "Derive new ways,/To uphold ignorance,/To keep slavery alive".

In Tiananmen Square
History repeats itself.

This final poem lacks the subtle freshness of the China poems of Oodgeroo's late fruition in September-October 1984. It brings her back to the harsh public world of political struggle.

Perhaps because of its peculiar publishing history, *Kath Walker in China* seems to have dropped from sight. The book is not widely known, and the poems have not been given much of a place in Oodgeroo's *oeuvre*. This is a pity. There is a scattered body of writing by Australians who have visited China, including memoirs, poems, translations, and some fiction. Very often such writings, nonfiction included, weave a line between recollection and imagination, fact and fantasy. Among poets whose work has drawn on China I could mention Harold Stewart, Randolph Stow, Rosemary Dobson, Fay Zwicky, Nicholas Hasluck and others. Oodgeroo's poems have a place in this company. At one level they document the kind of excited progress through China that so many thousands of Australians, from prime ministers to package tourists, made in the 1980s. At another level, they give utterance to the continuation of a long faint thread of Aboriginal Australian-Chinese relationship. Then they show a face of Oodgeroo that would not otherwise be seen. One appreciative reader, catching the sense of being thrilled that the poems convey, extended the poet's own metaphor to comment that Oodgeroo in China may have been "pregnant", and a little hysterically so, but her condition proved more fertile than any "hysterical pregnancy". *Kath Walker in China* shows Oodgeroo as a poet in her response to an extraordinary world. This is an especially valuable and lasting result of the 1984 cultural delegation. Judith Wright wrote to Oodgeroo in 1975, after Kath had sent her the poem "Sister Poet", encouraging her to go on writing, whatever else she did. "Keep writing;" urged Judith Wright, "it reaches more people than you'd think and we've only got one Kathy Walker."

WORKS CITED

Beier, Ulli, ed. *Quandamooka: The Art of Kath Walker*. Bathurst, NSW: Robert Browne Associates in association with the Aboriginal Artists Agency, 1985.

Walker, Kath. *Kath Walker in China*. Brisbane: Jacaranda P and International Culture Publishing Corporation of China, 1988.

NOTE

1 I am grateful to the surviving members of the delegation for so generously sharing their recollections of what was clearly a memorable experience: Dr Caroline Turner (then Launitz Schurer), Deputy Director of the Queensland Art Gallery, whose detailed official report on the visit is especially valuable, Dr Eric Tan and Rob Adams. I am also grateful for help and comments from Dymphna Clark, Dr Jocelyn Chey, Geoffrey Blainey, Sang Ye, Dr Geremie Barmé, John Collins, Dr Tamsin Donaldson and others; and for assistance from the staffs of the Fryer Library, University of Queensland (especially Margaret O'Hagan), the Cultural Relations Branch, Department of Foreign Affairs and Trade, and the National Library of Australia. I would also like to thank Professor Bruce Bennett and the English Department of University College at the Australian Defence Force Academy where, as a Visiting Fellow, I was able to write this account.

Poetry

The Poetemics of Oodgeroo of the Tribe Noonuccal

Mudrooroo

Poetry perhaps is whitefella business. In fact, I might declare that
I don't know one Aboriginal poet; that is, if I discount those
singer-songwriters such as Archie Roach, whose main mode of
expression is lyrical, and thus are close kin to our traditional singers
who sing about the cares and concerns of our communities and
countries. If I am pressed, however, I might say that I know one
Aboriginal person whose main mode of expression is in verse, and
that is Lionel Fogarty. Of course, I am narrowing "poet" down
to those whose main business is poetry, those who declare
themselves poets first and foremost, often from a nineteenth
century ideology of romanticism in which the person who
considered himself a poet was driven by divine inspiration to
versifying. The muse literally spoke (read: wrote) through him.
I use the pronoun "him" deliberately here, for there were few
women poets in the nineteenth century and naturally the muses
were seen as female, similar to Jung's anima: the inner woman.
   Oodgeroo, during my long friendship with her, never once
described herself as a poet. She often said, when pressed, that she
was an educationalist and that her job was to educate both white
and black; and so, I believe that to wrench her verse away from
her life and accepted role is to lose the message for the structure.
It is to lose the polemics by comparison with persons who have
described themselves as poets and are taken at this face value
through the filtering apparatus of a theory of aesthetics which
eschews the political — the polemical — for either the individual
or universal truth-utterance. In effect poetry, this kind of poetry,
is meant to be beyond the mundane utterance of the everyday,
or to engage in a transformation of the everyday into

the universal as exemplified by Alfred Lord Tennyson's "Flower in the Crannied Wall" or to engage in a fetishisation of language — to translate it into Keats's "a thing of beauty is a joy for ever".

I doubt that this last quotation could be used in regard to the verse of Oodgeroo, and thus my use of the term "poetemics" in the title of my paper, which is to separate social verses such as she wrote and recited from the more "serious" business of poetics which exists in and for itself, often as a "thing of beauty", of an aesthetic form which makes me recall those languorous female muses as depicted in Victorian paintings. "Poetemics" is coined from "poetry" (verse) and "polemics" in order to stress that what is important in the poems of Oodgeroo is the message and any aesthetic pleasure we derive from them is of secondary value. In fact, such poetemic verse may have the opposite effect and may repel those in search of an aesthetic. In such verse there may be a deliberate repudiation of aesthetic concerns in order to produce an alienation effect, akin to the theories of Bertolt Brecht in his search for a Marxist dramatics:

> True, profound, active application of alienation effects takes it for granted that society considers its condition to be historic and capable of improvement. True alienation effects are of a combative nature. (Willett, 277)

Such a repudiation of aesthetics and the resulting alienation may result in statements from critics such as this:

> She is no poet, and her verse is not poetry in any true sense. It hasn't that serious commitment to formal rightness, that concern for making speech true under all circumstances, which distinguishes Buckley and Wright at their best. *The Dawn Is at Hand* belongs more rightly to the field of social protest ... (Andrew Taylor, 1967)

Social protest is thus stated not to be the legitimate field of poetry, and though we might query this — especially in regard to poetry which stems from other than the European mainstream tradition — Oodgeroo's poetry from the first was labelled as "social protest" verse and was denied to be poetry. If this position is taken to be a negative judgement, then we are forced into attempts to rescue Oodgeroo for poetry, as may be seen in Cliff Watego's spirited defence at the Aboriginal Writers Conference in 1983 (*Aboriginal Writing Today*, 1985); but if we accept that Oodgeroo's verse is poetemical, then it needs no such defence and we are forced to heed the message rather than to drag her verse into the mainstream poetic tradition with all its aesthetic values.

Again, labelling Oodgeroo's verse as merely "protest" does have a limiting effect, as I have shown in my previous examination of aspects of her work in *Writing From the Fringe* (1990). Oodgeroo's poems do have a wide range of subject matter and often the "final protest" is left for the reader to make. This is not to say that overt protest is not found in Oodgeroo's verse. In *My People*, her constantly-reprinted collection of verse up to 1970, there are poems which rightly may be termed "protest" verse, such as "United We Shall Win" or "Intolerance"; but these are balanced by other poems such as "Bora Ring" and "Community Rain Song". These seek to impart nostalgia for the past and show aspects of Aboriginal culture, or hope for the future, or even statements about life in general. Her subject matter is wide and to dismiss all of her poems as being simply "protest" is naive to say the least.

Poetry is often judged on (as any recourse to reviews of poetry will show) an assumed originality or, if not, then a playful use of traditional forms — such as the ballad metre — which are often parodied. In contrast to these types, Oodgeroo's poetry is conservative in its experimentation with verse structures. She usually uses such verse structures as are part of the cultural unconsciousness of Australia. Here I include both non-Aboriginal and Aboriginal people as belonging to this cultural unconsciousness, with the proviso that Aborigines are included depending on their proximity to mainstream Australian culture and what they have had placed within their minds in that socialising and often assimilationist process termed "primary or tertiary education". Oodgeroo is included in this cultural unconsciousness because she did undergo such a formal process of socialisation and assimilation, as described in her story "Repeat Exercise" (*Stradbroke Dreamtime*, 1972) and as shown in her later involvement with the Realist Writers Group in Brisbane (pointed out by Cliff Watego). Owing to the conservative nature of both of these institutions, when Oodgeroo began writing verse, she favoured the ballad metre with its necessity of rhyme, though on later occasions she did use a type of free verse, as may be found in such poems as "Jarri's Love Song". In regard to the cultural unconsciousness of Australia, there is also the recourse to the structure of nursery rhymes (or children's play verses) in such poems as "No More Boomerang" which, rhythmically, appears to be based on "Here we go around the mulberry bush". I wish to stress here that we might not find a one-to-one correlation between a particular poem and a particular nursery or play rhyme. I doubt that the unconscious operates in this way, but more by way of allusion, or invocation. The formula, here being simplicity of rhythm and words, evokes simplicity of nursery or play rhymes which, in turn, evokes simplicity of a childhood state when such rhymes were heard or used. It is the invoking of this receptive state that prepares the mind for the reception of the message.

In poetemics, with the urgency of getting the message across to as many readers as possible, this of necessity includes those who do not read poetry and have become familiar with a few of its structures in schools; thus there must be recourse to what the adult learnt as a child. This usage of traditional structures is very important, for it invokes unconscious associations which cause a state of emotional rapport which may then be inclined to make the reader accept the message. I believe that structure is just as important, at least in this psychological regard, as is content and it played a large part in the ideology of the leftist (read: communist) realist writers' usage of verse structures which were familiar to the workers. It seems that Oodgeroo, through her membership of this group, learnt and then adopted this strategy. For her, it proved very successful. Her collected volume of poetry, *My People*, has never been out of print since it was first published in 1970 and still outsells all other Australian poetry.

But when such a strategy of using supposedly transcendent structures of poetry is adopted, there is a price to be paid. As Ruth Doobov has stated, "It is to be expected that her reviewer in the *Times Literary Supplement* should write: 'At times the metres of her poems are trite, stemming from the worst type of nineteenth century hymns.' This is undoubtedly true" (Doobov 49). Thus Oodgeroo's verse is placed outside the canons of what, for some, constitutes good poetry. And if we expect our poetry to be experimental and "flash", we will accept these criticisms as well-founded. Rhyming metrical verse, especially when read silently from the page, can seem trite and contrived and can even seem to unintentionally parody itself, at least under the eyes of those who are knowledgeable in poetic aesthetics. Simple rhyming schemes, as we find in much of Oodgeroo's verse, can make us grit our teeth, or smile disparagingly, or sink to condescension when reviewing them; but what we must not forget is that Oodgeroo never declared herself a poet's poet. She is writing, as she puts it in a 1977 interview with Jim Davidson in *Meanjin*, ". . . for her people"; and this must always be borne in mind, especially when we consider that most poetry published in Australia is completely ignored by much of the population. She, at the expense of contradiction in my paper, might be termed "a poet of the people" and what this means is that her poetry is easy to grasp and the messages come through loud and clear. The role of the educationalist is to use what tools are at hand and this she does.

Not only are the verse structures of Oodgeroo's poetry known to most Australians, but her language is also akin to Australian spoken language, although at times she does use an adaptation of Aboriginal English. The Australian English of Queensland is noted for its laconic flatness and lack of ornamentation and so is Aboriginal English. Thus, there is a noticeable absence of metaphor and simile in Oodgeroo's verse and an absence of "striking" images — which are supposed to be a feature of poetry. If this is so, how exactly does Oodgeroo's verse work? It works by the use of analogy and allusion, exactly as her verse structures seek echoes from the cultural unconsciousness. This is apparent in Oodgeroo's "No More Boomerang", one of her most popular poems which has been put to music on more than one occasion by Aboriginal musicians such as Coloured Stone. There are no similes in the short four-line rhyming stanzas, and the poem proceeds by invoking oppositions between the old ways of life of the Aboriginal people and the newly-arrived civilised ways. There is no attempt, except in the stanza on abstract art, to condemn outright; but it is left up to the reader, or listener, to draw out the conclusions. In its brevity and wit the poem is an example of Oodgeroo at her best. Again her style is proverbial, or aphoristic instead of image-based; and this laconic method, with its flat statements, is not what we are told good poetry is made from. In fact, her poem simply entitled "Verses" is a collection of aphorisms, or proverbs, which again is marked by no striking images; thus: "appearance is the world's test. Brother, you're treated as you're dressed."

From my foregoing discussion of aspects of Oodgeroo's poetry, it should be apparent that it is impossible to use mainstream poetic criticism to aid our understanding of Oodgeroo's verse and that we are in the presence of a different type of poetics, one which I have labelled "poetemic" in that the message value far outweighs any aesthetic concerns. Thus to judge her verse by the usual mainstream methods of seeking striking images and the clever use of other poetic devices would lead to her dismissal as a "poet". She declared herself an "educationalist" and what must be taken into account in any discussion of her written work is her success — or lack of it — in getting her message across. By any means of measurement, she has been most successful, as the sales of her books attest, as the number of her poems which have been put to music attest, and the number of her lines which are quoted. As an educationalist and a poetemist, she has fulfilled her role, and moreover has introduced poetry to those who otherwise would not have read it. The Alice Springs singer Ted Egan sings in relation to the Aboriginal fighter Tjandamara that "The people will decide"; and in Oodgeroo's case, they have decided in spite of those critics who condemned her verse outright.

WORKS CITED

Doobov, Ruth. "The New Dreamtime: Kath Walker in Australian Literature." *Australian Literary Studies* 6.1 (1973): 46-55.
Egan, Ted, ed. *Egan Presents the Kimberley.* Cassette recording produced by the singer, no date.
Meanjin, Aboriginal Issue. 36.4 (1977).
Narogin, Mudrooroo. *Writing from the Fringe.* Melbourne: Hyland House, 1990.
Oodgeroo of the Tribe Noonuccal, Custodian of the Land Minjerriba (published under Kath Walker). *The Dawn Is at Hand.* Brisbane: Jacaranda, 1966.
_____ . *My People.* Sydney: Angus & Robertson, 1972.
_____ . *Stradbroke Dreamtime.* Brisbane: Jacaranda, 1970.
_____ . *We Are Going.* Brisbane: Jacaranda, 1964.
Taylor, Andrew. Review of the *Dawn is at Hand. Overland* 36 (1967): 44.
Watego, Cliff. "Aboriginal Poetry and White Criticism." *Aboriginal Writing Today.* Ed. J. Davis and B. Hodge. Canberra: AIAS, 1985. 75-90.
Willett, John, tr. & ed. *Brecht on Theatre.* London: Methuen, 1964.

Poetry and Politics in Oodgeroo: Transcending the Difference

Bob Hodge

Politics has been described in many ways, most of them unflattering and all of them seemingly opposed to whatever poetry may be. Politics is the "art of the possible". As Kath Walker, Oodgeroo made Aboriginal literature possible in 1964 with the landmark publication of *We Are Going*. Politics in the Western democratic system is about getting the numbers. Oodgeroo's people do not have the numbers in Australia today but her poetry does. Her works have sold more copies than almost every other contemporary poet. Yet this kind of success which cannot be denied is in danger of being translated into a negative judgment on her value as a poet. Oodgeroo is "not a really great poet", the judgment goes. She is of historical interest, yes, that must be acknowledged. But that is all. She is history. But that proud judgment can erode her status as a poet, leading some to think of her as no longer a living poet whose words still count, whose poems can be read and reread with undiminished satisfaction by readers new and old.

In this article I want to argue against this profoundly unfair judgment, and expose the assumptions on which it rests. It is nothing new, of course. On the contrary it has dogged Oodgeroo's work like a shadow, like dirt that has been thrown over the words on her pages from the outset of her career, threatening always to discredit them and prevent them from reaching the readers that they have inspired for two generations now. In the 1960s and 1970s the sheer force of her work gained readers who did not need to justify or explain how they were reading her. In the 1990s the politics of Aboriginality has moved on, to new tasks that have become possible as a result of the great victories of Black activists of the '60s and '70s.

There has been similar development in the repertoire of stylistic options available to Aboriginal artists. In 1964 Oodgeroo was on her own, and she created the models that she chose. Today Aboriginal writing and Aboriginal art are arguably the most vigorous and innovative forces in the Australian cultural scene. In this new context it is dangerously easy to misread her work, to see it as good and necessary for its time but now somewhat limited in comparison with the sophistication and range shown by Aboriginal writers today. She can seem dated, a writer who is simple, artless and direct, formed by the artistic conventions of her time, which held her back because they were white not Aboriginal, but which have been transcended by those who have followed her. Or so this line of reasoning would have it.

With some diffidence I will use Adam Shoemaker's important study of Aboriginal writing as evidence that there is still a problem for judgment and interpretation to address for contemporary non-Aboriginal readers sympathetic to what Oodgeroo stands for. Shoemaker condemns some of the early white critics of Kath Walker's poetry. He quotes Leon Cantrell: "According to my system of pigeon-holes and prejudices she is not a poet. She has absolutely no feeling for words..." Andrew Taylor wrote in a similar vein: "She is no poet, and her verse is not poetry in any true sense" (Shoemaker 185).

Shoemaker condemns this as a "disturbingly limited critical position". He has no doubts about the importance of her work. However, he concedes that her work is "uneven" and has "technical weaknesses" (183). He defends such poems on the grounds of their "strong socio-political message", but this is tacitly conceding that the critique has force on aesthetic grounds. He does praise her free verse in *We Are Going*: "her free verse is often impressive in its directness and poignancy" (183). However, only 9 of the 30 poems in that book are in free verse, and being (often) "direct" and "poignant" is perhaps still different from showing the most highly prized qualities of literature. With admirable honesty Shoemaker states his own aesthetic judgment, that "she is not the most impressive or the most accomplished Aboriginal poet. Others have transformed Australian English into Aboriginal English in more innovative and exciting ways" (184).

It is not my purpose to criticise Shoemaker for articulating this

Signing copies of *My People*, Bathurst Island, 1964.

position. On the contrary, his well-informed, sympathetic and honest reaction is far more valuable than either ignorant condemnation or patronising praise would have been. Nor do I wish to engage in the un-Aboriginal and sterile (and increasingly obsolete) literary game of establishing who is the most impressive Aboriginal writer and who comes second, third and fourth, and who is or is not worthy to be included in the canon. What Shoemaker's comment shows is that it is still necessary to be clear about the literary qualities of Oodgeroo's poetry, because for all the seeming obviousness of her work these qualities still seem to be difficult to see and acknowledge.

The line of argument I want to pursue has been developed already by Mudrooroo (*Writing from the Fringe*, especially Chapter 3), who has insisted that Oodgeroo's work is far more ambiguous than it seems, open to multiple readings, multiple meanings and multiple judgments and evaluations. He situates her writing in the Fringe which is the situation of all Aboriginal writing, and in the context of the Fringe the judgments of the centre are complicated and inverted, even when they seem to be invited, as was the case with Oodgeroo's early work.

I return to those early negative criticisms quoted by Shoemaker, because the grounds of judgment are not yet safely out of date and irrelevant. Taylor's commentary, to quote it at greater length, went as follows:

> She is no poet, and her verse is not poetry in any true sense. It hasn't that commitment to formal rightness, that concern for making speech true under all circumstances, which distinguishes Buckley and Wright at their best. *The Dawn Is at Hand* belongs more rightly to that field of social protest in which Miss Walker's statements are most relevant and most moving. I have a sincere respect for her indignation, her sense of pathos, and her forthright candour. For any white Australian with a conscience her book is often moving and shaming. But to invite us to approach it as poetry is to invite us to take the easy way out, to avoid its message (for it is a book with a message) by measuring it against the standards and preoccupations with which it has really little to do. (Taylor 44)

It is apparent from this fuller quotation that Taylor is not hostile to the Aboriginal cause, and his distinction between poetry and protest is in fact (he claims) designed to give ''Miss Walker'' a stronger platform for her message to white Australians. In practice there is a contradiction here because he is so troubled by the issue of whether this is poetry that the political issues go into the background. But even so, he writes as a white liberal of the kind who in 1967, when he was writing, voted "yes" in the referendum. He is not seeking to avoid the message, but complaining about a problem he has with accepting the form in which it comes. His reaction, then, shows one positive political effect from the poetry, along with an element that tends to negate that effect. If he is accepted as being sincere he is declaring a painful inability to produce positive literary judgments about the poetry, and so he wishes that he did not have to produce any literary judgments at all.

The superior, dismissive tone he adopted towards the poetry outraged Mudrooroo, who as an Aboriginal writer has experienced the cumulative weight of continuous white patronisation. What he objected to is probably similar to what was put as follows by Denis Walker: "White people have the arrogant attitude of saying that their way of life, their white, western, straight-line way of thinking about how reality should be described is the only one" (McGuinness and Walker 50).

Things have changed within the world of literary criticism since 1967. Post-structuralism has come in with its own critique of the "straight-line way of thinking" of Taylor's absolutist aesthetic criticism and Cantrell's pigeon-holes. It has put in question the timeless certainty and recognisability of the qualities that make up the canon. It is now widely accepted that the "canon" was a particular construct, the reflection of the values and interests of a particular dominant group at a particular time, not the repository of an eternal set of ineffable truths that Taylor was able to appeal to in 1967. Where a phrase like "making speech true under all circumstances" sounded impressively vague and beyond criticism in 1967, now it sounds like gobbledegook or worse — as Mudrooroo for one has pointed out.

Aboriginal literature and art have been able to profit from the pluralist perspective of the new post-structuralist critical dispensation. Its difference is acknowledged as something that has a right to exist, and Aboriginal art no longer is compelled to conform to inappropriate European standards. However, the change is not as great as it might seem. Even in 1964 the critical chorus recognised that Aboriginal culture was based on different assumptions and traditions — though this came out in the negative form of a complaint that Kath Walker's poetry was not Aboriginal enough. Earnest white critics who claimed to understand Aboriginality better than she did said that they would have liked the work better if it had been more obviously Aboriginal. (See Shoemaker 182 for examples. For an extended critique of this tactic, termed ''Aboriginalism'', see Hodge and Mishra, Chapter 2.) Of course, in terms of these criteria she would not have been allowed to make political statements, in verse or prose, because that was incompatible with their normative Aboriginalist idea of what was Aboriginal. Her original work transgressed in two ways: it wasn't ''poetry'' and it wasn't ''Aboriginal''.

However, coming to the post-structuralist 1990s it can seem as though Oodgeroo has put herself outside the scope of a post-structuralist defence. Post-structuralism has its own aesthetic priorities, valuing free open forms over fixed forms, innovation over tradition, allusiveness over realism. In terms of this aesthetic it can seem that Oodgeroo was captured back in the 1960s, having opted for non-progressive forms for reasons that can be explained but which cannot save her from critical indifference and tacit rejection.

The formal choices that she made in the 1960s are still a problem in the 1990s, for many Aborigines as well as for non-Aboriginal critics. Mudrooroo (Chapter 3), for instance, expresses reservations about this aspect of her work, and that of Kevin Gilbert and Jack Davis, alongside other positive and insightful comments on how she uses these forms. The forms she predominantly chose seem to be non-Aboriginal and therefore can be suspected of being anti-Aboriginal, of betraying Aboriginality at the very moment she was seeking to proclaim it.

In order to address this issue directly I want to look at a widely-quoted and influential polemical statement by the American Black lesbian activist Audre Lord:

> *For the master's tools will never dismantle the master's house.* They may allow us temporarily to beat him at his own game, but they will never enable us to bring about genuine change. And this fact is only threatening to those women who still define the master's house as their only means of support. (Lord 112)

The slogan in italics proclaims the necessity for purity of style for all subjugated and oppressed peoples, a scrupulous and eternally vigilant avoidance of the contamination that would come from any use, however well intentioned, of the language or conventions of the dominant. Many Aboriginal writers have been impressed with this metaphor and have taken to heart the principle that Lord has proclaimed, however difficult it is to subscribe to it in practice.

Kath Walker changed her name to Oodgeroo Noonuccal, showing how aware she was of the dangers of cooption through language. The "white, western, straight-line way of thinking" that her son Denis Walker objected to is encoded in forms of language and in literary and other conventions, and it is enforced through judgments that claim to be neutral judgments of language and style. Oodgeroo would certainly not have rejected Lord's critical principle out of hand.

Nonetheless it is salutary to consider Oodgeroo's work as a whole in the light of Lord's words, and then to look again at the principle itself. For surely Oodgeroo did use the language of the master against him and beat him, as much as any Black writer has ever done, and she has been an agent of change that is deep and ongoing, not at all compromised by the way she waged her fight. She was a mighty warrior who in no way saw the master's house as her only means of support.

And if we look more closely at the metaphor it seems silly. At the literal level, some of the "master's tools" (sledgehammers, bulldozers, dynamite) could do a very good job of demolishing the "master's house" if that's what you want to do. It's the master's rules, not his tools that are the problem: starting from rule one, that the tools are his and should only be used as and when he directs.

Lord's metaphor makes better sense as an example of the genre of magical realism, a genre that is widespread in many areas of so-called "post-colonial writing". In these terms the master's tools can take on a life of their own, imbued with the values and the alienated will of the master opposed to those who use them — like the demonic buckets and brooms in Walt Disney's cartoon *Fantasia* or the animated kitchen utensils in the more recent Disney production *Beauty and the Beast*. Marx's eloquent account of the conditions of alienated labour is apposite for this nightmare form of consciousness amongst the dispossessed:

> The worker puts his life into the object and this means that it no longer belongs to him but to the object. So the greater the activity the more the worker is without an object ... The externalization of the worker in his product implies not only that his labour becomes an object, an exterior existence but also that it exists outside him, independent and alien, and becomes a self-sufficient power opposite him, that the life that he has lent to the object affronts him, hostile and alien. (Marx 135)

In Marx's analysis the sense of powerlessness before the master's tools is the result of alienation from powers whose origin is within the dispossessed themselves. The hostile magic that emanates from the master's tools is his last trick: using the energies of the dispossessed against them, and making it seem that these tools are part of his essential self and cannot ever be used against him. For those who have a sure sense of their own inalienable rights, their deep roots in their people and their land, the magic does not work. And Oodgeroo was such a one, confident and strong in her integrity, not disabled by the words and forms that she used, employing them in her own way to produce her own meanings.

This whole problem is an artefact of the simplistic binary thinking that is at the basis of racism. According to this reasoning, if something has anything to do with whites it can have nothing to do with Blacks. Similarly if it is poetry then it cannot be political, and if it is strong it cannot also be subtle and complex. Binary thinking is fundamental to Aboriginal culture too, but so also is an infinite capacity for enrichment and elaboration, so that the end product is exciting and unpredictable as well as showing respect for balance and symmetry — precisely the "serious commitment to formal rightness" that Taylor couldn't see in Oodgeroo's work.

To illustrate Oodgeroo's own kind of "serious commitment to formal rightness" I will look at "White Man, Dark Man" which is built around the duality that constitutes racism (*We Are Going* 19). The white man speaks first, addressing the dark man ("Abo man") in a complex stanza that is five lines and eighteen words long. The dark man replies in a stanza that is also five lines and eighteen words long, a perfect mirror image, like a dance, an image of the perfect justice between white and black that is not reciprocated as it ought to be from the other side. He picks up the phrase "social science" (white man's gift to Aboriginal people according to the white man, though Aborigines would not all see anthropology as either benign or scientific) and he transforms it to the "socialism" that Aboriginal people lived long before the white man came. "Democracy" is then repeated untransformed; another invention of the whites which Aborigines knew all about in their own traditional culture.

Formally speaking this is not only dance but also exemplary dialogue. The dark man listens precisely to the discourse that constructs him as other and different, lacking in the defining qualities of civilisation. Then he responds with a discourse of affinity, easily incorporating the alien words of political science into his dialogue or dance, gracefully evading the simplistic binary thinking of the white man within a formal binary structure of his own.

In the next verse the white man doesn't listen and respond to the dark man's argument but begins another one: an account of Aboriginal beliefs that reduces them to "ancestor Biami" and the "big bad/Bunyip and his bellow". This time his language is not white political discourse which is supposedly outside the range of "simple" Aboriginal people, but his own childlike version of Aboriginal language, as though he is confident that he can get down to the level of the dark man, and can use the "tools" of the dark man's cosmology against him in debate.

The dark man's response is intelligent and precise, not arguing against this caricature of his beliefs but offering a respectful version of Christianity, turned against the white man:

> You had Jesus Christ,
> But Him you crucified,
> And still do.

Christianity is economically invoked in eight words then used as a yardstick of the white man's hypocrisy in terms of his own beliefs. The pronoun "Him" is capitalised as in pious Christian discourse, and the values of Christianity are not repudiated in this text, which bites more strongly by endorsing them in this way. It is not, of course, outside Christian discourse to accuse the majority of the populace of crucifying Christ again by their indifference to the sufferings of their fellow humans. On the contrary, it is a recurring motif in Christianity with a basis in the Bible itself.

Oodgeroo constructs Christianity as a discourse that is not beyond her comprehension or destructive to her integrity. It is a tool that she can use with superb polemic skill, constrained by precision and respect.

I will take the opportunity here to comment briefly on the issue of poetic conventions and Oodgeroo's literary competence. "But Him you crucified" shows an inversion of the natural speaking order in English, something that Oodgeroo does often, and which contributes to the judgment that she is clumsy and old-fashioned in her diction ("absolutely no feeling for words" according to Cantrell, no ability to "make speech true under all circumstances" according to Taylor). A harsh judge could suppose that she inverted the order here simply to finish the line on the rhyme-word "crucified". This then creates the picture of someone whose language is determined by the demands of the form itself, who sacrifices her own meanings to the mechanistic requirement to end the line with a rhyme.

Of course, earlier poets in English used inversion and are not brusquely ejected from the canon for the crime. However, that tolerance comes from a recognition that inversion was accepted in these periods. It is not accepted to the same extent now in poetry. But paradoxically this means that inversion in the past signalled conformity to expectations of poetic discourse. Oodgeroo's use of inversion is not so sanctioned now, which makes it disturbing, subversive, an assertion to her rights over a broader range of poetic conventions than contemporary white poets feel they can avail themselves of. At the same time inversion corresponds to a quality of Aboriginal languages compared to English, their greater freedom of word order. Oodgeroo's use of poetry to legitimate her departures from "natural" spoken English is subtly subversive and invisibly Aboriginal.

The last line shows how much she is in control of this resource. The rhythm of this line breaks with the iambic metre she has used to this point in the poem to end with the powerful double blow of two consecutive stressed syllables, three syllables to the line where the rest have six. Oodgeroo is good at strong endings, and this is no exception. This poem is organised both as a dance, in which a movement one way is balanced exactly by a movement in the other direction, and as a linear progression, an argument that goes from one place and moves a long way to a powerful climax. To use Denis Walker's terms this shows "white straight-line thinking" and it is indeed as straight as a spear that finds its target. But linearity is not un-Aboriginal or outside the scope of Oodgeroo. On the contrary, she moves easily between both and she is in total control of the terms of that movement. This is how the master's tools are best used.

Binaries weave their way through her poetry — black and white of course, but also then and now, anger and hope and wealth and poverty. Because she was such a powerful fighter on behalf of her Aboriginal people she is liable to be cast into a one-sided position, but that would be un-Aboriginal, and in practice her poetry shows in a modern form the traditional Aboriginal genius for creating harmonious and complex patterns out of opposing elements. It is this quality that has been most underestimated in her work, which makes it more various and complex and hard to pigeon-hole: more "post-modern" and at the same time more true to the primary values of Aboriginal tradition.

For the critical tradition in which Cantrell and Taylor were formed, a high value was given to a sense of the individual "voice" of a poet, and they found Kath Walker wanting in this respect ("one can gain no notion of the individual person behind the verse", Cantrell). Aboriginal writers, including Oodgeroo, are very concerned with the category of "voice" and they see it as an important part of their poetic mission to give their people a voice. In Oodgeroo's words:

> I'm putting their voices on paper, writing their things. I listen to the Aboriginal people, to their cry for help — it was more or less a cry for help in that first book, *We Are Going*. I didn't consider it my book, it was the people. ("Interview" 429)

One difference here is that the individual voice that Cantrell sees as the sole indicator of authenticity is not Oodgeroo's major concern. This aesthetic decision is based on two political contexts and agendas, both Aboriginal, overlapping in some ways but very different in others. One constructs the socially-embedded individual of traditional society, who does not seek to be different from the rest of the group in the way that Cantrell requires of his poets. The other produces the multiplicity of responses and strategies that constitute the irreducible diversity of Australian

Aboriginal peoples, but which is reduced to a unitary concept of Aborigines by the ideological processes of what I have termed Aboriginalism which were then used to condemn Oodgeroo's work.

We can see something of the complexity involved in the title of Oodgeroo's first work. "We Are Going", as the reader first meets it, is inflected with the militant, confident persona of Kath Walker, Aboriginal activist, and it seems to promise that she and her people are on the move, they are going places. As in truth they were. But the phrase is also the title of a poem and the last line of that poem, where it is given a very different inflection and context. There it is in quotation marks, the final despairing words of some Aborigines, "All that remained of their tribe", who see the last vestiges of their culture disappearing before the destructive advance of white "civilisation". "'The corroboree is gone./And we are going'". It is a "cry for help", precisely as Oodgeroo described it.

But this context does not negate the original reading of the phrase "We Are Going" in the title, as a positive battle cry. The experience of dispossession is felt intensely and painfully by the group who are the speakers in the poem, and Oodgeroo gives it eloquent expression, but she is also the powerful speaker of "Aboriginal Charter of Rights", the opening poem in the book. The belief that the Aboriginal "problem" would be solved by the dying away of all the Aboriginal people was the comfort of Australian racists for a century, so that the aim of the notorious policy of assimilation was constructed as "soothing the dying pillow", in the famous words of Daisy Bates (1938). Oodgeroo did not believe that hypocritical lie. She knew that in spite of all that they had suffered and were still suffering Aboriginal people were growing stronger, not weaker, and that they were not about to disappear quietly from the Australian scene. So the title has a double meaning and a double authorship: a desperate cry from a dispossessed people and a rallying cry from a people on the move, united in the "we" which includes the unassimilably contradictory experiences of both.

A major part of her poetic work went into the construction of this complex "we", this emerging, contradictory and shifting Aboriginal subjectivity which incorporates suffering and hope, anger and goodwill. Her poems typically state or imply a speaker and an addressee. Most often they are a dialogue from an Aboriginal perspective to a white addressee. Sometimes the speaker is an individual, an "I" who is Aboriginal and woman, drawing on personal experience to address whites from a position of confidence and strength: the Oodgeroo persona "I am black of skin among whites"). At other times the speaker is "we", a collective pronoun speaking on behalf of Aboriginal people ("We want hope, not racialism").

Grief and optimism coexist within single poems, contradictions held together by the fluid boundary around the "we" who is continuously being created. For instance the poem entitled "United We Win" calls the black man "one of a dying race" in its second line. How could someone who is part of a dying race be united and able to win? The answer lies in the shifting configurations of the "we" who is/are capable of many alliances and experiences without jeopardising a fundamental unity of identity.

Oodgeroo's work in constructing her complex Aboriginal persona is complemented by her work in constructing an object of her address. From the point of view of understanding the political effectiveness of her poetry this is perhaps her most subtle and important quality.

Some of her poems address other Aborigines, either individuals or collectivities, her "people". In these poems a white reader is positioned as a privileged hearer, admitted into the exchange which constitutes the poem, tacitly welcomed into Aboriginal society itself. It is an effective tactic for overcoming the prejudice of white readers.

However, the majority of her poems address white readers directly and polemically. This is why they are experienced by many of those readers as uncomfortable; as "protest" works, not poems. She made it difficult for her readers simply to feel good and do nothing. Tactically it was a risk, since it could have alienated those readers, who had the power of all readers not to read, to close the book and continue to think their racist thoughts.

In spite of the risk, the tactic worked. Her poetry engaged with white people, challenged and transformed them. That is no small achievement for a poem, and it is worth inquiring how she did it. The secret was the place she constructed for her white reader, as complex as the Aboriginal places she constructed from which to speak. She explicitly excludes some whites from her condemnation of white actions ("the good white hand stretched out to grip the black": "United we win"). She also addresses whites as capable of shame and self-correction. In "Whynot Street", for instance, she first described the "feeble yes-men" who signed a petition against "abos" in Whynot Street. But then she addresses whites as follows:

And are we still the ousted, then,
And dare you speak for decent men?
This site was ours, you may recall,
Ages before you came at all.

The "you" is the site of intersection of the racists of Whynot Street and the reader, and the structure of "you" is as fractured as the structure of her Aboriginal "we". The racists are constructed as an anomalous insertion into the mass of "decent men" for whom they have no right to claim to speak. Non-Aboriginal readers, then, have a choice. They can acquiesce in the claims of the racists of Whynot Street to speak for them, or they can repudiate their racism and injustice, and accept Oodgeroo's more positive construction of them as "decent" people who have knowledge of the past and are willing to act on that knowledge. They become "the White Australian with a conscience" whom Taylor claimed to speak for, in the critique which showed him in the process of accepting the place she had assigned him.

Oodgeroo's polemic address, then, is designed to miss its target, or to strike merely a glancing blow, allowing white readers to evade the designated reading position in one way or the other. One way of putting it is to say that she appeals to their "better" (non-racist, egalitarian) nature, but it is also the case that she is constructing this better self, a white person who is both racist and potentially decent, responsible for or implicated in the crimes of the past but also committed to justice for all, especially for Aborigines. This new self is constructed in the act of reading, coerced to choose to disidentify with "typical" Australians while not being offered the choice of supposing it possible to become an honorary Black.

The complexities of this tactic and of the reading position that she has constructed directly reflect the political complexity of the situation that she was writing in. Political and aesthetic qualities grow out of precisely the same source. It is for this reason that there is not an opposition between her poetic and her political purposes, or between the value of her work from the two perspectives. Her poetry is more varied, subtle and complex than it has been seen to be, more postmodern and more Aboriginal, and all of this because her political experience was wider and her political sense more nuanced and better developed than some have given her credit for. Oodgeroo was not simply the first Aborigine to publish a book of poems; she laid down a legacy that was broad enough to encompass a wide range of possibilities for those who followed her. If this fact is not recognised then not only will justice not be done to her work, but it will be deprived of some of its power to inspire and teach Aboriginal writers of today and tomorrow.

WORKS CITED

Bates, Daisy. *The Passing of the Aborigines*. London: Duckworths, 1938.
Hodge, Bob, and Vijay Mishra. *Dark Side of the Dream*. Sydney: Allen and Unwin, 1991.
Lord, Audre. *Sister Outsider*. New York: Crossing P, 1984.
Marx, Karl. "Economic and philosophical manuscripts." *Karl Marx: Early Texts*. Ed. D. McLellan. Oxford: Blackwells, 1971.
McGuinness, Bruce, and Denis Walker. "The Politics of Aboriginal Literature." *Aboriginal Writing Today*. Ed. Jack Davis and Bob Hodge. Canberra: Australian Institute of Aboriginal Studies, 1985.
Mudrooroo. *Writing from the Fringe*. Melbourne: Hyland House, 1990.
Noonuccal, Oodgeroo (Kath Walker). *We Are Going*. Brisbane: Jacaranda P, 1964.
_____ . "Interview." *Meanjin* 36.4 (1977): 428-41.
Shoemaker, Adam. *Black Words, White Page: Aboriginal Literature 1929-1988*. St Lucia: U of Queensland P, 1989.
Taylor, Andrew. Review of *The Dawn Is at Hand*. *Overland*, 36, May 1967: 44.

Long Memoried Women: Oodgeroo Noonuccal and Jamaican Poet, Louise Bennett

Angela Smith

In my country

walking by the waters
down where an honest river
shakes hands with the sea,
a woman passed round me
in a slow watchful circle,
as if I were a superstition;

or the worst dregs of her imagination,
so when she finally spoke
her words spliced into bars
of an old wheel. A segment of air.
Where do you come from?
"Here," I said, "Here. These parts." (Kay 24)

Jackie Kay's country is Scotland but she can be demonised within
it because she is black. The poem's narrator has to assert her right
to the land which does not itself erect barriers (the river shakes
hands with the sea) in the face of a woman who wants to enclose
her within the familiar bars of the old wheel that has been rolling
since the first colonial encounter. The weary final line suggests
the familiarity of the situation, and reminds the reader of the
ambiguity of the title of Sally Morgan's *My Place*, as both assertive
and alert to the implications of knowing one's place and what
others assume it to be. Oodgeroo encapsulates it in a phrase in
her poem about Willie Mackenzie, whom she describes as a
"Displaced person in your own country" (*My People* 12). Kay
claims her own space by writing herself into it, as Oodgeroo claims
her people's unassailable right to their ancestral territory and their

place in contemporary Australia in her poetry. The British preoccupation with hierarchy, race and class, which was part of the mental baggage of the first invaders of Aboriginal land, is still alive and well where it began. As Oodgeroo says of the settlement of Australia:

> I think you have to go back to the early times, when England, which has a lot to answer for, sent all those people out here...I think they still have that psychological hang-up of not wanting to be at the bottom of the totem pole, the bottom rung of the ladder; so they're deliberately keeping the Aboriginals down. (Baker 292)

In *Writing from the Fringe* Mudrooroo makes an implicit comparison between Oodgeroo and African writers:

> Oodgeroo Noonuccal espouses for the Aboriginal writer a far different role than that espoused by conventional Anglo-Celtic writers. If we need search for comparisons we might look towards African literature which appears to be concerned with people rather than self...all aspects of traditional Aboriginal culture were part of a holistic concept of society and to demand an antisocial place for an artist was undreamt of. Art was a social act. (23-24)

The same comparison is made in Mudrooroo's poem "Art":

> Taking art into their lives,
> Thinking it gave beauty,
> Taking art into their lives:
> Oh, African beauty,
> Our tracks crisscross,
> Meet, part, cross again...
> Ever-seeking unconsciously for what makes our world entire.
> (*The Song Cycle of Jacky* 76)

The comparison is an interesting one, focussing as it does on the social imperative that controls the writer, her role within her community, and her function as healer. It is particularly relevant to the African diaspora, where people of African descent are either in a minority, as in Britain, or were disempowered by their position as slaves, as in the Caribbean. Emmanuel Nelson suggests similar links when he writes that "there emerges a pattern of defeat, dispossession and denigration in the historical character of all black experiences" (Nelson 3), as Kevin Gilbert does in his introduction to *Inside Black Australia*. The need to contest denigration and rewrite history is implicit in the title to this article, taken from the cycle of poems by the Guyanan poet Grace Nichols, *i is a long memoried woman*.

Women are familiar with the fact that their knowledge is habitually discredited by societies with masculinist values, a masculinism often linked with nationalism in post-colonial societies:

> Nationhood is so bound up in textuality, in "definitive" histories and official languages and mythologies, that to compose a substantially different kind of text, using vernacular forms that are part of people's experience, is already to challenge normative discourses of nationhood. (Nasta 10)

It is perhaps not surprising then that the dynamism and originality of Oodgeroo's poetry should be parallelled by another woman, in Jamaica, with the insight to recognise the value of her own indigenous culture, unpopular as that view was when she began to write. Louise Bennett was born in 1919, a year before Oodgeroo; she too was part of a self-fracturing process that invited black people to define themselves as contemptible:

> "When I was a child nearly everything about us was bad, you know; they would tell yuh seh yuh have bad hair, that black people bad...and that the language yuh talk was bad. And I know that a lot of people I knew were not bad at all, they were nice people and they talked this language." (Bennett iii-iv)

The language in question is Jamaican Creole, which Velma Pollard describes as "a Creole of English lexicon which everyone in the speech community understands. Because of the lexical relationship between the two languages most Creole speakers regard themselves as English speakers" (Nasta 239). Bennett's antecedents were African slaves who were prevented from speaking their own language by being separated from those of their own community when they were deported and sold. As early as 1807, Robert Renny's *History of Jamaica* records anonymous songs in Jamaican Creole, evidence of the slaves' resistance to the dehumanising attempt to silence them. Oodgeroo describes a similar but even more tragic process when she records the death of the Noonuccal language; her people were flogged at school for using it, and only a few words remain. Her own work was the first to inscribe

Aboriginal English in poetry, the syntactical structures as well as the language often asserting difference and appropriation:

> Bunyip he finish,
> Now got instead
> White fella Bunyip,
> Call him Red. (*My People* 33)

Part of the discredited knowledge, transmitted in a discredited language, of both Noonuccal and Jamaican people was their stories and folklore. Oodgeroo and Louise Bennett were pioneers in recording an endangered oral tradition. What Paula Burnett writes of Bennett applies equally to Oodgeroo, both of them working in a cultural climate hostile to their endeavours:

> Realizing that the stuff of poetry was all around her in the drama of ordinary people's lives and in the language which they spoke, she began to write and perform...She is a serious folklorist who has done more to promote respect for ordinary people and their culture than any academic could have done. (Burnett xxxix-xl)

The word "folklore" has the wrong connotations in English for the vigorous process involved; another populariser of his people's stories, the Ugandan poet Okot p'Bitek, rejects the word as an "elitist, restrictive and discriminatory definition" whereas he wants a "dynamic and democratic definition" (p'Bitek 20).

The work of Bennett and Oodgeroo is so dynamic and democratic that both of them were for years excluded by an elitist, restrictive and discriminatory definition of poetry. In *The Independence Anthology of Jamaican Literature* published in 1962, Bennett's work was placed in the "Miscellaneous" section, rather than under poetry, and in 1964 Oodgeroo's *We Are Going* was dismissed as propaganda, used as a pejorative term: "It may well be the most powerful social-protest material so far produced in the struggle for aboriginal advancement...But this has nothing to do with poetry" (qtd. Shoemaker 182). Oodgeroo's indictment of that attitude had already been written, in her poem "Aboriginal Charter of Rights", deploying the bite of the rhymed couplet satirically:

> Though baptized and blessed and Bibled
> We are still tabooed and libelled.

You devout Salvation-sellers,
Make us neighbours, not fringe-dwellers. (*My People* 36-37)

Similarly, Bennett defends herself indirectly against the claim that her dialect poems exclude her from serious consideration as a poet in "Bans a Killin".[1] The speaker asks "Mass Charlie" about the news that dialect is to be killed:

Yuh will haffi[2] get de Oxford Book
O' English Verse, an tear
Out Chaucer, Burns, Lady Grizelle
An plenty a Shakespeare!

Wen yuh done kill "wit" and "humour"
Wen yuh kill "variety"
Yuh will haffi fine a way fi kill
Originality! (5)

The uncertainty and condescension with which the work of these two poets was approached is evident from the physical appearance of the first edition of *My People*, with its shoddy illustrations, caricaturing the suffering that is explored in the poems. On the page opposite "All One Race", for example, a merry colonial officer, with a pith helmet over his eyes and a flower between his teeth, sits on an igloo(!) embracing a native American; at the bottom of the same page a kangaroo sheds a tear. The comparison with the powerful illustrations for *Father Sky and Mother Earth* done by Oodgeroo herself is poignant. Though she was an artist before she became a writer, when it came to illustrating her own book "my white Australian publishers didn't even ask me to do it...I was very upset about it when I saw it...it looks like a send up of *Alice in Wonderland*. I'm very disappointed about it" (Rutherford 24). Part of the wariness seems to stem, in both cases, from the fact that Oodgeroo and Bennett are entertainers. They produce poems that are intended to be read aloud, and to benefit from it. The poets identify themselves with their own oral traditions. In both cases these are ones in which the audience participate, and through them the outlook and values of the people are conveyed pleasurably or emotively. Though the traditions differ radically, they are inclusive and communal.

In the Caribbean, work and dance songs were used to posit an alternative politics to that imposed by the masters, and to tell stories that suggested methods of subversion. Their creators inherited and utilised a particular inflection of an African oral tradition of irony and satire. This could be found, for instance, in what were apparently praise songs in which the griot sang about a chief, which in fact often criticised the leader's failings and made them public. Another function of songs within the African tradition is to transmit grievances and gossip; a woman singing a pounding song to her companions who provide a chorus may want the village elders to overhear and find out how badly her husband treats her. Louise Bennett's poems, most of them dramatic monologues, use topical events and local news to interrogate social and political issues with an apparent naivety. The speaker often speculates innocently about current local news, but the poem communicates ironically with its audience, for instance in the use of "motherlan" in "Colonisation in Reverse":

> What a joyful news, Miss Mattie;
> Ah feel like me heart gwine burs —
> Jamaica people colonizin
> Englan in reverse.
>
> By de hundred, by de tousan,
> From country an from town,
> By de ship-load, by de plane-load,
> Jamaica is Englan boun.
>
> Dem a pour out a Jamaica;
> Everybody future plan
> Is fi get a big-time job
> An settle in de motherlan. (106)

What Bennett says of the Jamaican folk custom of singing what is known as a "dinky" to the family of a dead person applies to her own work and Oodgeroo's: "when you look between the lines you find all the sorrow there and all the facts too, but if you don't search for it, if you don't care, well then you won't find it." (xvi). Her credo might also link her with Oodgeroo: "I believe in laughter". The cheerful, bouncing rhythm of Oodgeroo's "No More Boomerang" belies its topic, a lament for a lost way of life in the vernacular, with a constant ironic thrust, as in "higher" for "hire":

No more boomerang
No more spear;
Now all civilized —
Colour bar and beer.
. . . .
No more gunya,
Now bungalow,
Paid by higher purchase
In twenty year or so.
. . . .
Lay down the woomera,
Lay down the waddy.
Now we got atom-bomb,
End *every*body. (Oodgeroo 32-33)

The particular irony of the final stanza lies in the fact that Woomera as well as an Aboriginal weapon is also a missile testing station, with a US tracking station nearby.

The use by both poets, in the passages quoted, of the ballad form, with an emphatic rhythm and consistent rhyme scheme, suggests the similarities in their education, though both vary the form and metre of their poems. Both quote directly and indirectly from the Bible, and the metrical patterns of hymns are echoed in their verse. One of the disjunctive experiences for the reader/hearer is the gap between the orthodoxy this suggests, and the challenge offered to it by the content. The mythos of Christianity and of both different oral traditions is at odds. The totems in Oodgeroo's poetry perform functions that have no equivalent in Christianity. The curlew's cry, for instance, is an omen of death, and the curlew itself leads the spirit away:

Three nights the curlew cried. Once more
He comes to take the timorous dead —
To what grim change, what ghastly shore? (4)

Obeah and myal, both forms of witchcraft, permeate Bennett's poetry; taken individually, the poems may seem to mock the superstitions of the speaker, but collectively they communicate a sense of a spirit-world inhabiting tangible reality which cannot be controlled by Christian religious practices. Erna Brodber's novel *Myal* suggests that Christianity and myal are not necessarily inimical, but that the myal man works through plants, trees, insects and creatures to counter the effects of obeah. The speaker in Bennett's "Rollin-Calf" is in a hurry to rescue Tahta John from the rollin-calf, a monster that takes the form of a calf with fiery eyes and haunts the roads at night. However, he stops to pass on the gossip, constantly saying that he can't stop:

> Me cyaan tap — is a obeah man
> Dem sen me fi go fetch;
> Me feel me yeye a jump — him mighta
> Dead before me ketch. (37)³

Duppies (ghosts) fill the landscapes that Bennett's characters inhabit, as they fill the poet's awareness of the present in *My People*. In "Understand, Old One" the poet is with archaeologists when they excavate a burial ground near Brisbane, and feels anxious that she may seem sacrilegious:

> Understand, old one,
> I mean no lack of reverence.
> It is with love
> I think of you so long ago laid here
> With tears and wailing.
> Strongly I feel your presence very near
> Haunting the old spot, watching
> As we disturb your bones. Poor ghost,
> I know, I know you will understand. (68)

In *Writing from the Fringe* Mudrooroo defines the Aboriginal writer as "a Janus-type figure with one face turned to the past and the other to the future while existing in a postmodern, multicultural Australia in which he or she must fight for cultural space" (24). One aspect of this function for Oodgeroo is to suggest to a white Australian readership the possibility that snakes are not intrinsically evil, in spite of the story of the Garden of Eden which informed the settler culture. In *Stradbroke Dreamtime* she tells the story of the Rainbow Serpent, and in "Ballad of the Totems" she plays her two worlds off against each other, as the title suggests. The rollicking rhythm and rhyme, and the frame of reference, show the poet's familiarity with western writing:

> You should have heard her diatribes that flowed in angry torrents
> With words you never see in print, except in D. H. Lawrence. (*My People* 24)

The story told is an ambivalent one; the narrator and her family have lived at close quarters with a huge carpet snake. Her father protected it because it was his totem, and all the children were used to its presence in the house, and its habit of slithering across the floor at night, in search of chickens. Her mother hated it because it ate her hens. The pivotal point in the anecdote is the cause of the snake's disappearance. The elders say that it disappeared in sympathy with the father's death, as "It was his tribal brother", but the poet's suspicions are less mystical. Her mother looked smug and they "all had snake for tea one day about that time". The ability to inhabit two worlds is clear in the phrase "had snake for tea", but the tensions and contradictions in the position are evident in the scepticism in this poem compared with the seriousness of a poem like "Community Rain Song". The persona that develops through the juxtaposing of the poems is a complex one, which contradicts itself and sometimes seems to mock the gullibility of the reader. The element of the trickster in this is also part of the tradition Bennett recorded and explores in her work, the Ananse figure which Edward Brathwaite defines as "the spider-hero of the Akans; earthly trickster, but once with powers of the creator-gods" (Brathwaite 272). He is comparable with Esu-Egbara in the Yoruba pantheon, and is connected with subversion and disruption. Bennett's poems are full of anecdotes about pretentious middle-class people who are made to look foolish, or about people in power whose status is deflated by the speaker, as when Sir John Huggins became governor of Jamaica:

> What a way dem gwan bout new Governor,
> Jessa meck whole heap a fuss.
> Dem a gwan like him is rare steak
> Or any tree-month war bonus.
> . . . .
> De way dem all go dung[4] fi meet him
> All dress up eena silk
> You hooda[5] tink him is a whole
> Big tin a condense milk. (26-27)

Bennett and Oodgeroo prioritise the voices of ordinary people. Oodgeroo said of *We Are Going*: "It was more a book of their voices that I was trying to bring out, and I think I succeeded in doing this...I'm putting their voices on paper, writing their things" (qtd. Shoemaker 186). The relevance of this to Bennett is obvious. Mervyn Morris tells how she began to write, after getting on a tram dressed in her best clothes:

> On the electric tramcars...people travelling with baskets were required to sit at the back, and they were sometimes resentful of other people who, when the tram was full, tried to join them there. As Louise was boarding the tram she heard a country woman say: "Pread[6] out yuhself, one dress-oman a come." (iv-v)

She went home and began her first dialect poem with the words "Pread out yuhself deh Liza". Both Bennett's and Oodgeroo's poems are read most rewardingly not individually but as whole polyphonic texts, speaking with the voices and moods of their communities. Mudrooroo's insists that "this type of poetry, utterly 'committed', expresses what poetry (at least in Western literary theory) should not do, that is give a situational, social and political importance to the genre" (*Writing from the Fringe* 38). This importance becomes clear when the collections are read as a whole, the poems interacting with each other and gaining from what Mudrooroo calls "retroactive reading" which involves "a reviewing, a revising, a comparing backwards and forwards as the structure is decoded" (54).

The texts by Bennett to which I have access were compiled into categories by critics, so that the specific juxtaposition is not hers, but the overall impression of the poems is cumulative. Themes that express the community emerge through the forms of the poems; what seems a joke in one poem gains in significance through variation and repetition. The comic interaction in "Bed-Time Story" between an English nursery rhyme and gossip, as a mother tries to get her child off to sleep and chat to her friend at the same time, is entertaining:

> Mary had a little lamb
> — Miss Mattie li bwoy Joe
> Go kick May slap pon har doorway —
> His feet was white as snow. (6)

As the poems continue to intersect with British literature, the reader gains an increasing sense of interference, even though the original is parodied, as Charles Wolfe's "The Burial of Sir John Moore at Corunna" is here, in "Independence Dignity":

Not a stone was fling, not a samfie⁷ sting
Not a soul gwan bad an lowrated⁸;
Not a fight bruck out, not a bad-wud shout
As Independence was celebrated. (116)

What kind of independence it is going to be becomes a question.

The role of women in Jamaican society is explored and celebrated in the poems; many of the speakers are tough women who ridicule pretensions. In ''White Pickney'' the speaker suggests that, as the British are shipping the babies of black fathers and white mothers out of Britain to America, their GI fathers' home, Miss Mary should send her mixed race baby (pickney) off to Britain, where his father comes from:

An now yuh sure seh dat him white
Yuh cyaan raise de pickney,
For him naw go able fit eena
Yuh black society. (99)

This assertive and ironic reversal of racial prejudice is complemented by mockery of people who want to pass as white, and an attempted redefinition of ''nayga'' (nigger) as a term of praise rather than abuse, though the connotations of the word are so strong that this is not altogether persuasive. Accompanying the poems of political awareness and street wisdom are others that reveal hardship and the mystification that stems from a colonial education designed to keep the colonial subjects in their place. Sue, who calls herself a nephew instead of niece, sends her aunt an account of the coconut-growers' meeting which she attended because her aunt's tree had blown down in a hurricane. The apparently naive letter reveals the intervention of a new breed of capitalists in what was a rural area:

Bans a big-shot money-man was deh.
Some a dem get out cross
An start fi talk bout omuch hundred
Tousen tree dem loss.

Me did meck up me mine, Aunt Tama,
Fi get up an talk free,
Fi touch dem pon dem consciance
Meck dem gi yuh back yuh tree.

But when me hear de man-dem mout

> Dah gwan like distric bell
> Me heng me head, fole up me wing
> An draw eena me shell
> ....
> De chairman cough an blow him nose.
> "Thank you madam," him seh.
> De tarra⁹ man-dem look pon me
> Like me no business deh. (87-88)

Here the woman is put in what is deemed to be her place by another Jamaican; a wide variety of women and men speak through the text, with one voice reflecting on, and modifying, another. A poignant and persistent sense of poverty and hardship pervades the collection, expressed forcefully in poems like "Dutty Tough", but with it there is a celebration of the vitality and ingenuity of the language: a "pass de riddim coat" is one which hangs below the buttocks, or the rhythm section.

Social issues related to women are given priority in *My People*; "Dark Unmarried Mothers" focusses, as Bennett's "White Pickney" does, on black mothers with mixed race babies, but in Oodgeroo's poem the tone is overtly angry, exposing the invaders' cruelty, and their indifference to the Christian moral criteria that they have imposed on Aborigines:

> No one to protect them —
> But hush, you mustn't say so,
> Bad taste or something
> To challenge the accepted,
> Disturbing the established.
> Turn the blind eye,
> Wash the hands like Pilate. (8)

The phrase "bad taste or something" pinpoints Oodgeroo's link with Bennett; neither will be silenced ("hush, you mustn't say so") by the pressure to mimic a hypocritical and alien model of behaviour. The emphatic repetition of these lines as a kind of refrain is not in poetic good taste either, but movement from anger to pleading to laughter, through a range of other moods, creates a flexible but recognisable voice which does not conform to any kind of orthodoxy. It attacks the mores of its own people when they seem unjust, as in "The Child Wife", and sometimes expresses uncertainty and a sense of inferiority:

White superior race, only time is between us —
As some are grown up and others yet children.
We are the last of the Stone Age tribes,
Waiting for time to help us
As time helped you. (21)

This obviously conforms to a colonial paradigm of parent culture,
mother country, with the colonised as permanent children or
adolescents. What Oodgeroo has the courage to show is that the
indoctrinated must have moments when they feel themselves to
be what they have insistently been told they are; she contradicts
this view in many other poems, but shows that we do not always
know what we know. At other moments she shows confidence and
authority, as in this memorable trope in "Assimilation — No!":

Pour your pitcher of wine into the wide river
And where is your wine? There is only the river. (22)

One of the most powerful moods evoked in *My People* which
has no equivalent in Bennett's work is something much stronger
than nostalgia, a longing and to some extent a lament for a way
of life. On the page opposite the optimistic and assertive "United
We Win" the reader finds the elegiac poem "We Are Going",
the juxtaposition suggesting how difficult it must be to maintain
a fighting stance when despair threatens to engulf the embattled
consciousness. "We Are Going" uses a form, familiar in many
oral traditions, of repetition with variation, its dwindling line
lengths enacting the waning of the life described; the reader is
reminded of the ghosts that haunt the text, as many of the poems
celebrate dead members of the Noonuccal tribe. The poem takes
on the commemoration of the people with the dwindling of the
ancient rites:

We are the quiet daybreak paling the dark lagoon.
We are the shadow-ghosts creeping back as the camp fires burn low.
We are nature and the past, all the old ways
Gone now and scattered.
The scrubs are gone, the hunting and the laughter.
The eagle is gone, the emu and the kangaroo are gone from this place.
The bora ring is gone.
The corroboree is gone.
And we are going. (74)

Though the long-memoried woman has herself gone now, her poems remain. Jackie Kay's poem about Bessie Smith is a tribute to "a woman's memory" and its role in history:

> In the early
> light, the delicate bone-light
>
> that broke hearts, a song swept from field to field;
> a woman's memory paced centuries,
>
> down and down, a blue song in the beat of her heart,
> in an old car that crossed
>
> a railroad track; the scream of a warning —
> is that why we remember certain things and not others;
>
> the sound of the bass, the sound of the whip, the strange
> strangled wind, bruises floating through light air
>
> like leaves and landing, landing, here; this place.
> Everything that's happened once could happen again. (Kay 9)

WORKS CITED

Baker, Candida, ed. *Yacker 2*. Sydney: Pan, 1987.

Bennett, Louise. *Selected Poems*. Kingston: Sangster's Book Stores, 1983.

Brathwaite, Edward. *The Arrivants*. Oxford: Oxford UP, 1973.

Burnett, Paula, ed. *The Penguin Book of Caribbean Verse*. Harmondsworth: Penguin, 1986.

Kay, Jackie. *Other Lovers*. Newcastle upon Tyne: Bloodaxe, 1993.

Narogin, Mudrooroo. *The Song Cycle of Jacky*. Melbourne: Hyland House, 1986.

———— . *Writing from the Fringe*. Melbourne: Hyland House, 1990.

Nasta, Susheila, ed. *Motherlands: Black Women's Writing*. London: Women's P, 1991.

Nelson, Emmanuel S., ed. *Connections*. Canberra: Aboriginal Studies P, 1988.

Oodgeroo Noonuccal, (as Kath Walker). *My People*. Milton: Jacaranda, 1970.

p'Bitek, Okot. *Africa's Cultural Revolution*. Nairobi: Macmillan, 1973.

Rutherford, Anna, ed. *Aboriginal Culture Today*. Sydney: Dangaroo P, 1988.

Shoemaker, Adam. *Black Words, White Page*. St Lucia: U of Queensland P, 1989.

NOTES

1 bans a: lots of
2 haffi: have to
3 "I can't stop — they sent me to fetch an obeah man; I can feel my eye twitching — he might be dead before I can find the obeah man." A twitching left eye is a bad omen.
4 dung: down
5 hooda: would have
6 pread: spread
7 samfie: confidence man, trickster
8 lowrated: badly behaved
9 de tarra: the other

Oodgeroo: Orator, Poet, Storyteller

Anne Brewster

The past and history have been foregrounded in Aboriginal consciousness as issues that demand attention whereas the history of white Australia has often been taken for granted. Because they are a minority group Aboriginal people's history was, until the 1960s, invisible within the white community. As Klaus Neumann has observed (284), poetry may function as history, and in this article I examine in Oodgeroo Noonuccal's writing the emergence into print of an Aboriginal history. As a child Oodgeroo Noonuccal lived a semi-traditional way of life and like many of her generation she witnessed the passing of that lifestyle. Her writing negotiates this loss and in the phases that her relationship with the past and history undergoes, we can chart various constructions of Aboriginality from the 1960s onwards.

Noonuccal's writing falls into two phases. The first encompasses the 1960s when she worked with various activist groups, primarily FCAATSI. This period saw the publication of her first three books of poetry, *We Are Going* (1964), *The Dawn Is at Hand* (1966) and *My People* (1970). The second phase corresponds chronologically to Noonuccal's return to and residence on North Stradbroke Island (Minjerriba) from 1971 onwards. During this period she produced mainly prose apart from the collection of poetry, *Kath Walker in China* (1988), and miscellaneous poems in journals, magazines and books. Her first book of prose was the collection of stories, *Stradbroke Dreamtime* (1972). This was followed by several books of legends and drawings, some of which were designed for children: *Father Sky and Mother Earth* (1981); as well as *The Rainbow Serpent* (with Kabul Oodgeroo Noonuccal) (1988), *Australian Legends and Landscapes* (1990) and *Australia's*

Unwritten History (1992). Ulli Beier edited a book of her artwork, *Quandamooka*, in 1985. Most of her writing and drawings in these texts relate to her homeland of Minjerriba.

These two phases, with their focus on different genres and political issues, are demarcated to a certain extent by the ways Noonuccal names herself. It seems appropriate to maintain the name Walker with reference to the early poetry and to use the name Noonuccal — which she assumed on the eve of the 1988 Australian bicentennial "celebrations"[1] — when referring to her later work. For general or summarising comments about the writer and her work I will use the name she chose in preference to "Kath Walker" as it is appropriate to acknowledge the political reasons for this choice.

Noonuccal's role throughout both phases of her writing career is similar to that of the storyteller or singer who, in traditional Aboriginal cultures, played a crucial role in accessing history and sustaining Aboriginal culture. For example, as Catherine H. Berndt has pointed out:

> because Aborigines were traditionally non-literate, fundamental instructions and information about [the land and its resources] came through words, in word-of-mouth transmission — not so much through drawings, cave paintings and visual symbols, but predominantly through *words*, spoken and sung: stories and songs were a major means of transmitting and sustaining Aboriginal culture. (93)

Storytelling and song are oral modes and traces of orality inform the different genres Noonuccal used. This orality varies in form according to the genre. My focus is primarily on her poetry, or what I have called the first phase of her writing.

The poetry of Noonuccal's first three books thematically depict either dispossessed and detribalised Aborigines or the idyllic past. Some poems in the former category have commonly been referred to as "protest poems" because of their description of suffering and their call for justice in sometimes exhortative language. It is this particular genre of poetry which interests me here; I propose that the enunciative voice of Walker's "protest poems" enacts the traditional role of the storyteller/singer/orator.

I would like to look at the first poem in *We Are Going*, "Aboriginal Charter of Rights". The poem appears opposite the book's opening dedication which invokes Article 1 of the United Nations' Declaration of Human Rights: "All human beings are born free and equal in dignity and rights ... and should act towards one another in a spirit of brotherhood." Walker read the poem at the fifth Annual General Meeting of FCAATSI (to which body the book is dedicated) in Adelaide in 1962. In an interview she describes the situation which gave rise to the poem:

> [It] was written because we were then fighting to wipe out the Queensland Aborigines and Torres Strait Islanders Act. We claimed that under the Charter of Rights all people were born free and equal and we were entitled to the same thing. When we took our case to people like Pat Killoran (Queensland State Government official) their answer was that because the Native Affairs Act had been written long before the United Nations Charter of Rights, it takes precedent [sic] over the Charter. Therefore, the Aborigines and Islanders *have* no Charter of Rights. (Qtd. Watego, "Backgrounds" 18)

Noonuccal's commentary goes some way towards explaining why an Aboriginal Charter of Rights would have been so significant to Aborigines at this time and why the response to her reading of the poem at the meeting was so emotional. She recalls how, after a stunned silence, "every black man and woman was on their feet saying, 'I want a copy'. And I was frightened. 'What have I done?' I thought" (Watego, "Backgrounds" 14).

This anecdote is significant as it describes Noonuccal's charisma as both a writer and an orator; it is her role as a leading spokesperson and public speaker of the 1960s, I would argue, that enacts some aspects of the storyteller or singer's role in traditional Aboriginal society.

An Aboriginal leader in the 1960s was necessarily first and foremost a speaker. The oratorical skill of "Aboriginal Charter of Rights" is evident. It is an energetic and rousing manifesto whose iambic tetrameter invokes the marching rhythm of protest rallies, and whose powerfully interrogative penultimate lines underscore Aborigines' frustration over the fundamental injustices of the pre-1967 Constitution. The poem draws on the language of bureaucracy, the Enlightenment rhetoric of the Declaration of Human Rights, the Bible, and slogans of black militancy. The insistent repetition of binary opposites names both the injustices of the past (for example, Aboriginal people were "serfs on

Oodgeroo in 1957.

stations'' and the white settlers ''slavers'') and the reforms that were needed. The repetition of ''not'' in almost every line creates a powerful effect of refusal and resistance.

The orality of Walker's poetry enacts a de Certeau-like tactic of ''poaching'' in the discourses of colonisation and control (de Certeau 37). In her poetry Noonuccal appropriates those discourses (such as I have listed above) which impinge upon and circulate within the lives of Aboriginal people. Her engaging with the official discourses of governmental bureaucracy represents an intervention into and a rewriting of these forms. It was discourses such as the Queensland *Aborigines and Torres Strait Islanders Act* (mentioned in the interview cited) which named Aborigines and constructed their subjectivity. They were defined, for example, as wards of the state, to be ''protected'' and ''assisted''.

It is significant that most of the genres of the Western literary tradition which Noonuccal has appropriated are fundamentally oral. Indyk (255-56), for example, lists American protest songs, Lawsonian ballads, nursery rhymes and liturgical forms among these genres. The poem ''Oration'', which was presented to FCAATSI ''for use in the oration, Parliament House, Canberra, Friday, March 27, 1970'',[2] demonstrates Walker's borrowing from Christian oral recitation. In its use of the vocative voice in addressing the spirits of her ancestors, repetition, the subjective mood in such phrases as ''May your spirits go with us'', and its solemn and elegiac mood, the poem draws on the genre of Christian prayer. Walker assumes the position of the minister or priest leading her congregation in prayer; the ''church'' is Parliament House, the seat of white government and authority which is defamiliarised in the poem as ''the invaders' talk-talk place'', a site on which Aboriginal people are the ''strangers'' but which they reclaim by invoking ''the unhappy past'' which has been suppressed in white history and memory, and by giving voice to ''the cries of [its] unhappy people''.

It has often been observed that Aboriginal writing foregrounds its political agenda and is committed to social and political issues (e.g. Narogin 24). After the 1960s Noonuccal became proud of the political agenda and social commitment of her poetry which she describes as ''sloganistic, civil writerish, plain and simple'' (Walker, ''Aboriginal Literature'' 39). In answer to a question as to how she responded to charges of being a didactic and propagandistic writer[3] she replied: "I agreed with them because it *was* propaganda. I deliberately did it" (Noonuccal "Recording the Cries" 19).

It is hardly surprising, however, that the oral and performative nature of Noonuccal's poetry and its political agenda were the very features which drew criticism from critics. Early reviews of *We Are Going* and *The Dawn Is at Hand* commonly assessed her poetry according to the conventions of canonical lyric poetry and, naturally enough, found it lacking. The effect on her early writing of this kind of criticism with its divorce of high art from popular and political life is recorded in the Foreword to *The Dawn Is at Hand* where Noonuccal writes:

> My good friend and best critic James Devaney who taught me much, suggested to me that "propaganda-like stuff" which might be all right for my campaigning addresses on behalf of Aboriginal Advancement is not necessarily good in poetry. So in the present book the only poem of the kind (I think) is the ballad "Daisy Bindi".

Given the enormous general interest in Walker's first book, the patronising response of academics to the cultural phenomenon it represented was an indication of the academy's isolation from major political and cultural shifts of the period.

In the field of Australian Studies, Walker's poetry raised the issue of what it might contribute to the project of constructing a national literature. The question, "has [Walker] contributed anything distinctively Aboriginal to Australian Literature?" was posed (Doobov 46). In his re-invoking and positing of an answer to this question Adam Shoemaker points to the orality of Noonuccal's early poetry (180). We can go one step further, I would suggest, and affirm the continuity of this orality in Aboriginal culture.

Noonuccal demonstrates this continuity not only in her role as a spokesperson and poet but also in the material she uses; in the Foreword to *The Dawn Is at Hand*, for example, she writes: "Neither are the old tribal tales here my own invention, but were heard from the old people when I was a child." Therefore, rather than seeing the arena of Australian Studies being enlarged or expanded by the entry of Aboriginal texts, it is more pertinent to speak of two different discourses or traditions existing side-by-side and intersecting at the moment marked by the appearance of the Aboriginal storyteller in print.

In what I have called the second or prose phase of her writing, Noonuccal develops further her interests in traditional tribal lore. Her storytelling assumes the form almost exclusively of a chronicler of legends. In her several collections of legends she both records tribal stories from her own land of Minjerriba and collects others from elsewhere. Additionally, in the second half of *Stradbroke Dreamtime*, she devises her own stories and myths about her tribal homeland.

The storytelling tradition of Aboriginal culture was still strong in 1990 when, in her Foreword to *Australian Legends and Landscapes*, Noonuccal described the Aboriginal leaders of the time as orators: "I hope this book will help put the record straight and that the present generation of the white Australian invaders will at long last start listening and learning some of the truths from the orators within the Aboriginal tribes" (8).

Noonuccal's reading of the land can be seen as one of the definitive characteristics of her Aboriginality. Although this issue became predominant in her later prose writing, there is evidence of it in her early books of poetry. These books to a large extent present an image of Aborigines as detribalised and dispossessed: in many of the poems they are seen as victims of white racism and this sense of victimisation is emphasised by Walker's attitude of deference to white society. She asks whites for tolerance, help, assistance, sympathy and compassion, thus positioning Aborigines as helpless, childlike and subordinate.

Kevin Gilbert identified in this experience of powerlessness in the 1960s and 1970s the historical experience of shame: "Much of this shame survives today. It can be seen in the poetry of Kath Walker who, though feeling that her ancestors were inferior to the clever white man, nonetheless struggles to identify herself with the underdog" (5).

Despite the resistance to and rewriting of official discourses that we see in her protest poetry, Walker had to some extent internalised the subjectivity that white bureaucracy had constructed for Aborigines and the early poems reflect in part the rhetoric of the assimilationist policies of the 1950s and 1960s, as Rask Knudsen

(1991) has suggested. Her depiction of Aboriginal culture shows the loss of a past idyllic way of life and the passing of traditional Aboriginal culture. In presenting Aborigines as detribalised and dispossessed, she suggests that their Aboriginality lay in their spiritual relationship with the land. The poetry is characterised by the tragic doubt that it might be impossible to retain these links with the land if the older generation were "dying out" and taking with them the spiritual heritage of Aboriginality.

The poetry articulates the crisis of Aborigines in the 1960s negotiating the loss of traditional culture. There is an awareness that history has not recorded the voices of past generations as the titular poem of the first book of poetry, "We Are Going", suggests. A silence inhabits the poem: the tribal people amid the detritus of white culture's rubbish dump are without words: "They sit and are confused, they cannot say their thoughts." What follows is ventriloquism in which the poet "speaks" these people. Her voice, however, does not articulate their thoughts so much as her own relationship to these people and the past. This relationship is one of loss but also of discovery; she witnesses these people and her ancestors in the land — in the lightning, the thunder, the daybreak and the shadows. The list of the aspects of nature in which they are embodied is in the present tense. The repetition of the phrase "we are ...", which culminates in its completion, "we are going", places emphasis not only on the final word "going" but also on the reiterated word "are": the final effect is one of emphasising the presence of the tribal people as much as their absence.

Aboriginal people are still present in the landscape in spite of being dispossessed of their land. Their sense of alienation from the land (which symbolises the ventriloquist/poet's alienation from them and the past) is revealed to be in fact an illusion of loss and disappearance; the preposition "as" in the first line of the ventriloquism, "We are as strangers here now, but the white tribe are the strangers", is telling. Despite their dispossession they are not in fact strangers in the landscape at all, nor is the poet estranged from them and the past (that is, from her own Aboriginality); it is in fact "the white tribe [who] are the strangers". So this poem, which would appear to be mourning the passing and "dying away" of Aboriginal culture, in fact affirms the continuity of Aboriginality through the poet's reading of the land.

We can see in this early poem a trace of the preoccupation with the land that was to dominate Noonuccal's archival collection of tribal legends from the 1970s onwards. This theme is picked up, for example, in the story "Oodgeroo" from *Stradbroke Dreamtime*. Like the dispossessed people of "We Are Going" who "cannot say their thoughts", the woman in "Oodgeroo" is without words; she longs for the "stories" of her lost tribe. She finds an entry into these stories, and is therefore able to assert the continuity of her Aboriginality, through an identification with nature — this time with the paperbark trees: "when next the paperbark-trees filled the air with the scent of their sweet, honey-smelling flowers, they took her into their tribe as one of their own" (80). Once again the land symbolically enables the articulation of the continuity of Aboriginality.

Despite the fact that early poems like "We Are Going" illuminate the landscape with the memory of past generations, the feeling of the loss of traditional culture threatens to overpower their affirmation. Pathos is the dominant mood of many of these early poems. There is, nonetheless, a growing sense of anger at urban and industrial encroachment. Protest poems such as "Whynot Street" and "Acacia Ridge" bitterly lament the powerlessness of the Aboriginal people to keep their homes and to resist white incursion on their land.

The issue of land rights, however, did not dominate the political struggles of the early 1960s. When Walker wrote her "Aboriginal Charter of Rights" in 1962, the rights that she was demanding were almost entirely abstract (such as brotherhood, equality, freedom, self-reliance, self-respect, fellowship, love, opportunity, choice, goodwill and incentive). Although there are a few specific political reforms named (for example, as relating to education, housing and citizenship), land rights did not figure among them. Land was nonetheless clearly a definitive feature of Aboriginality for Walker, even though Aboriginality was something she, at that stage, apparently located in the traditional culture of the past rather than in the lifestyle of her own generation.

Although her third book, *My People*, reprinted many of the poems from the two earlier collections, some of the newer poems such as "Time Is Running Out" indicate a rejection of the pathos of the earlier poetry and an intensified sense of protest. If in the early poetry the Aborigines' spiritual bond with the land was depicted largely in relation to the traditional Aborigines who were "going", "Time Is Running Out" changes the focus of loss and also the strategy with which to combat it. In this poem it is the land itself that is threatened and the encroaching mining industry is identified as the enemy. Time is running out then, not simply for the traditional Aborigines and their way of life, but for the conservation of the land, which itself was to become the central issue in Noonuccal's later writing. The poem is a forerunner to the land rights issues that dominate her prose from the 1970s onward, and found an ally in the white discourse of environmentalism.

It is interesting to note the distinct change of tone in "Time Is Running Out". No longer are Aborigines portrayed as the helpless and frustrated victims of white society; rather they are exhorted to recognise that their love for the land is "violent" rather than mournful and grieving, and to "show strength" and "take a stand". The militant tendencies in this exhortation, however, are carefully modified with the suggestion that they are essentially, and must remain, "gentle" in spite of this "violent love":

> Come gentle black man
> Show your strength;
> Time to make a stand.
> Make the violent miner feel
> Your violent
> Love of land.

We can thus see in Walker's protest poetry of the 1960s, framed in my discussion by the first and penultimate poems of these three books, both resistance and compliance to the assimilationist policies of the period. Tim Rowse has suggested that, given the history of the institutionalisation and surveillance of Aboriginal people, in mapping their recent history we should be sensitive to their "transitions out of welfare paternalism and into 'self-determination'" (53). Bearing in mind Rowse's cautioning (in his use of quotation marks for the phrase "self-determination"), I would suggest that Walker's poetry of the 1960s articulates precisely this kind of transition.

I would like, finally, to pick up the relationship of writing to orality. The decision to work with the written word was a conscious political decision for Noonuccal. She describes in an interview how old Aboriginal men would express themselves at public meetings through the Bible, and that the sight of this prompted her to write them "a book they could call their own" ("Recording the Cries" 18). She describes seeing, after the publication of *We Are Going*, the same old man who used to quote the Bible, reciting her poetry at a meeting, despite the fact that he could neither read nor write; he had got his white friends to read it to him and had memorised it (23).

This anecdote suggests that recitation and oration have an important role in Aboriginal society and that as a poet Walker stepped into the shoes of the traditional storyteller, singer or orator. The book is a vehicle for the storage and transmission of orally instructive texts; in one of its first appearances in Aboriginal culture it enabled the words of an Aboriginal storyteller/ singer/orator to circulate in a wide arena and introduced a sense of solidarity or common interest among Aboriginal people which allowed some degree of pan-Aboriginality to develop for the first time.

Noonuccal concluded her anecdote about the old man and how *We Are Going* replaced the Bible, with an explanation for the popularity of the book: "for the first time the Aboriginals had a voice, a written voice" ("Recording the Cries" 19). Her comment that it was crucial at this time that Aborigines had not only "a voice" but "a written voice" attests to the importance of print as a medium for facilitating the national or pan-Aboriginal consciousness that arose out of Aboriginal people's struggles against colonisation. Noonuccal's choice of the phrase "written voice" rather than "written word" indicates that for her the process of publishing poems, many of which had been written for performance (such as "Aboriginal Charter of Rights" and "Oration"), was a process more akin to the transcribing of an oral text than the adoption of an entirely new mode of (writing) thought.

In one of her collections of legends she describes the legends as "our unwritten history, told over and over around the camp-fires" (*Australia's Unwritten History* 5). While this method of sustaining Aboriginal culture functioned well, in the past, Noonuccal's commitment is clearly to transforming that unwritten history into a written one. This is not to say that the oral practices will not continue, as it surely will in both domestic and public arenas, nor that "Aboriginal experience ... can shift unproblematically from the spoken tradition to the available western written genres" (Muecke "The Scribes" 46). Muecke elsewhere observes that there is a common view that "the spoken word [is] giving way to the more powerful written word and disappearing into the depths of time" ("Aboriginal Literature" 27). I would argue on the contrary, like Muecke, that oral "literature" (such as song, storytelling and oration) is alive and well and that, in fact, orality informs and shapes much contemporary Aboriginal (written) literature. While the written word has been important to Noonuccal in writing and disseminating her poetry, the poetry itself has its roots in indigenous performative and oratorial practices of the storyteller and singer.

Another way of depicting the historical continuity of Aboriginal oral "literature" might be firstly to reformulate our notion of writing, as do the editors of *Paperbark*: "In a broader sense writing is definable as any sort of meaningful inscription, and in the case of Aboriginal Australia this would include sand paintings and drawings ... body markings, paintings as well as engravings on bark or stone" (Davis et al. 3); and secondly, to reformulate our notion of literature as Muecke does: Aboriginal literature, he suggests, spans "Radio Redfern in central Sydney to initiation ceremonies, from the lyrics of country and western songs to the *Djanggawul* song cycle of Arnhem Land" (Muecke, "Aboriginal Literature" 27).

At the first Aboriginal writers' conference at Murdoch University in 1983 several people interrogated the term "literature" in these ways. Denis Walker, for example, stated that "any expression of that Aboriginal culture is literature, black literature" (McGuinness and Walker 50). Thus, while it is often said that the publication of *We Are Going* marked the beginning of Aboriginal literature (see, for example, Beston 446), I would suggest that, although the book undoubtedly had widespread repercussions as one of the first Aboriginal texts to appear in print, it is also fruitful to see Noonuccal's writing as part of a continuum of Aboriginal cultural production which extends from the traditional orator, singer and storyteller to the contemporary activist and writer.

WORKS CITED

Anderson, Benedict. *Imagined Communities.* 1983. London: Verso, 1991.

Beier, Uili, ed. *Quandamooka: The Art of Kath Walker.* Bathurst, NSW: Robert Brown & Associates in association with The Aboriginal Arts Agency, 1985.

Berndt, Catherine H. "Traditional Aboriginal oral literature." *Aboriginal Writing Today.* Ed. Jack Davis and Bob Hodge. Canberra: Australian Institute of Aboriginal Studies, 1985. 91-103.

Beston, John. "The Aboriginal Poets in English: Kath Walker, Jack Davis and Kevin Gilbert." *Meanjin* 36.4 (977): 446-62.

Davis, Jack, Stephen Muecke, Mudrooroo Narogin, and Adam Shoemaker, eds. *Paperbark: A Collection of Black Australian Writings.* St Lucia: U of Queensland P, 1990.

de Certeau, Michel. *The Practice of Everday Life.* Berkeley: U of California P, 1988.

Doobov, Ruth. "The New Dreamtime: Kath Walker in Australian Literature." *Australian Literary Studies* 6.1 (1973): 46-55.

Gilbert, Kevin J. *Because a White Man'll Never Do It.* Cremorne: Angus & Robertson, 1973.

Indyk, Ivor. "Assimilation or Appropriation: Uses of European Literary Forms in Black Australian Writing." *Australian Literary Studies* 15.4 (1992): 249-60.

McGuinness, Bruce, and Denis Walker. "The Politics of Aboriginal Literature." *Aboriginal Writing Today.* Ed. Jack Davis and Bob Hodge. Canberra: Australian Institute of Aboriginal Studies, 1985.

Mudrooroo. "A Literature of Aboriginality." *Ulitarra* 1 (1992): 28-33.

Muecke, Stephen. "The Scribes." *Meridian* 14.1 (1985): 41-48.

_____ , Jack Davis, and Adam Shoemaker. "Aboriginal Literature." *The Penguin New Literary History of Australia.* Ed. Laurie Hergenhan, Bruce Bennett, Martin Duwell, Brian Matthews, Peter Pierce, and Elizabeth Webby. Harmondsworth: Penguin, 1988. 27-46.

Narogin, Mudrooroo. *Writing from the Fringe.* South Yarra: Hyland House, 1990.

Neumann, Klaus. "A Postcolonial Writing of Aboriginal History." *Meanjin* 51.2 (1992): 277-98.

Noonuccal, Oodgeroo. *Stradbroke Dreamtime.* 1972. Pymble: Angus & Robertson, 1992.

_____ . "Recording the Cries of the People." Interview with Gerry Turcotte. *Aboriginal Culture Today.* Ed. Anna Rutherford. Sydney: Dangaroo P, 1988. 17-30.

_____ . *Australian Legends and Landscapes.* Milsons Point: Random House, 1990.

_____ . *Australia's Unwritten History.* Sydney: Harcourt, Brace, Jovanovich, 1992.

_____ , and Kabul Oodgeroo Noonuccal. *The Rainbow Serpent.* Canberra: Government Printing Services, 1988.

Rask Knudsen, Eva. "Fringe Finds Focus: Developments and Strategies in Aboriginal Writing in English." *European Perspectives: Contemporary Essays on Australian Literature*. Ed. Giovanna Capone, Bruce Clunies Ross, and Werner Senn. St Lucia: U of Queensland P, 1991.

Rowse, Tim. *After Mabo: Interpreting Indigenous Traditions*. Melbourne: Melbourne UP, 1993.

Shoemaker, Adam. *Black Words, White Page: Aboriginal Literature 1929-1988*. St Lucia: U of Queensland P, 1988.

Walker, Kath. *We Are Going*. Brisbane: Jacaranda, 1964.

⸻ . *The Dawn is at Hand*. Brisbane: Jacaranda, 1966.

⸻ . *My People*. Brisbane: Jacaranda, 1970.

⸻ . "Aboriginal Literature." *Identity* 2.3 (1975): 39-40.

⸻ . Interview with Jim Davidson. *Meanjin* 36.3 (1977): 428-41.

⸻ . *Father Sky and Mother Earth*. Brisbane: Jacaranda, 1981.

⸻ . *Kath Walker in China*. Brisbane: Jacaranda and International Culture Publishing Corporation of China, 1988.

Watego, Cliff. "Aboriginal Poetry and White Criticism." *Aboriginal Writing Today*. Ed. Jack Davis and Bob Hodge. Canberra: Australian Institute of Aboriginal Studies, 1985. 75-90.

⸻ . "Backgrounds to Aboriginal Literature." *Connections: Essays on Black Literatures*. Ed. Emmanuel S. Nelson. Canberra: Aboriginal Studies P, 1988. 11-24.

NOTES

1 For her statements relating to this name change see "Poet swaps name in protest", *Sydney Morning Herald* 16 December 1987: 3 and "Why I am now Oodgeroo Noonuccal", *Age* 30 December 1987.

2 Published in *Origin*, April 1970: 2.

3 See for example reviews in *Times Literary Supplement* (Thursday September 10, 1964: 842) and *Australian Book Review* (May 1964: 143).

From Kath Walker to Oodgeroo Noonuccal? Ambiguity and Assurance in My People

Eva Rask Knudsen

Biame told her to go to the paperbark-trees and ask them to give her some of their bark ... The woman sat down and drew from her bag the charred pieces of sticks she had taken from the dead fires, and placed the paperbark flat upon the ground. She drew the sticks across the paperbark, and saw that they made marks on its surface ... And when the next paperbark-trees filled the air with the scent of their sweet, honey-smelling flowers, they took her into their tribe as one of their own, so that she would never again be without the paperbark she needed for her work. They called her Oodgeroo. (*Aboriginal Culture Today* 31-32)

My copy of *My People* — a 1986 reprint — has a photograph of Kath Walker on the cover. She sits on a rock at the edge of a pool looking thoughtfully past the fixed frame of the photograph. Her figure is mirrored in the water. She evidently poses for the camera and allows it to capture a neat, placid and harmonious image of a Europeanised Aboriginal woman in nature. And yet, at a second glance the look in her eyes may be full of restrained patience rather than calmness; of quiet, pondering the next move, rather than ease. In contemporary Australia Aboriginal politics have evolved in many ways around the crucial symbolic act of naming, and in the bicentennial year of 1988 Kath Walker made the very determined move of changing her name to Oodgeroo Noonuccal as both a rejection of Europeanisation and an assertion of cultural self-hood. Her new name identified her with paperbark, her functional dreaming as chronicler of her people's stories.

Although purely incidental, the double image of the poet — the real and the reflection — featured on the cover of *My People* echoes through a reading of the poems in which two distinctly different voices speak. One is apparently accommodating to white expectations of Aboriginal adaptation to — and possible merging with — European culture, as in "Let Us Not Be Bitter":

> Life is change, life is progress
> Life is learning things, life is onward.
> White men had to learn civilized ways,
> Now it is our turn.
>
> . . . .
>
> The past is gone like our childhood days of old,
> The future comes like dawn after dark,
> Bringing fulfilment. (2)

The other is defiant and intent on differentiating black aspirations from white norms as in "The Past":

> Let no one say the past is dead.
> The past is all about us and within.
> Haunted by tribal memories, I know
> This little now, this accidental present
> Is not the all of me, whose long making
> Is so much of the past
>
> . . . .
>
> Deep chair and electric radiator
> Are but since yesterday,
> But a thousand thousand camp fires in the forest
> Are in my blood.
> Let none tell me the past is wholly gone.
> Now is so small a part of time, so small a part
> Of all the race years that have moulded me. (93)

This confuses the reader who is eager to know, if not to frame, the speaking position of the poet. Which one is her true voice? As *My People* comprises poems written over at least a decade of crucial political developments in Aboriginal affairs[1] one might see the two voices as epitomising a personal process of maturation that turned Kath Walker into Oodgeroo Noonuccal. However, a reading of available interviews with the poet and activist in which she comes across at *all* times as a devout freedom fighter who wants to keep white society at a manageable distance refutes such a proposition. This ambiguity then should be examined beyond its surface layers and seen as a deliberate strategy. This would suggest that any perceived deference to white society is really a tactical move, and that Kath Walker was in fact Oodgeroo all the way through her outstanding achievements in life.

Seen in retrospect it is interesting that many white critical evaluations of Oodgeroo's poetry have been caught between what Hodge and Mishra (1990) term "Aboriginalism" on the one hand and political correctness on the other, whereas black critics like Mudrooroo (1990) insert apparent contradictions into a general discussion of the psychology of the fringe, in which ambivalences found in Aboriginal writing seem to take on a more productive meaning. This essay will discuss the inscriptions that Oodgeroo made on her paperbark from these two critical perspectives and conclude with the idea that Oodgeroo made strategic use of the enigmatic double voice.

Aboriginalism may be defined as a complex discursive system of divide-and-rule imposed on Aboriginal people — whether consciously or not — and controlled in this case by mainstream critics who prescribe "who can speak about what in what way . . . and with what authority" (Hodge and Mishra 26). It is basically a tactical device which, with great affection, situates the *real* Aborigines within the mystical domain of the Dreaming and constructs the Aboriginal person from there as an otherworldly and much desired "other" to the white imagination that controls the image. Accordingly, critics have approached Oodgeroo's poetry on the lookout for a serene, unequivocal Aboriginal voice of primordial essence and found it wanting when measured against their already set standards of authenticity and purity. Her poems were accessible enough to become popular and, once popular, were easily dismissed as too accessible because Aboriginalism gives "high cultural status to an almost complete inability to read Aboriginal meanings at all, in the name of Aboriginality" (Hodge and Mishra 74). As Oodgeroo used, primarily, simple rhymed verse forms and wrote in standard English this, of course, resulted in foreseeable criticisms like "she is not a poet . . . one can get no notion of the individual qualities of the person behind the verse" (*Poetry Magazine* 1 [1967]: 31) and "the authentic voice of the Aboriginal song-man (sic) using the English language still remains to be heard" (*Australian Book Review* May 1964: 143). A songmaker by this implication is someone who confers upon the white critical audience something of the "primitive" mysticism of an organic pristine culture which is so much in demand by members of the critical school of Aboriginalism. This, however, never was Oodgeroo's world or her preoccupation. Her art is in no way "otherworldly"; it pivots around the crucial issue of survival: "My People face dispossession, disease and death," she says (*My People* 47), a grim predicament that allows for neither "the luxury of a single consistent position" (Hodge and Mishra 75) or idle reflections on cultural purity. In a callous sort of final analysis Aboriginalists do not find that black deaths or profound rapes of soul make compelling poetry, just as the confusion of bewildered and outraged voices speaking from this world of instability are deemed "impure" because *the* singular Aboriginal voice is supposed to be transcendental and beyond the reality of grass-root politics (a fallacy to which I shall return).

It is a great tribute to Oodgeroo, who is one of Australia's topselling poets, that she remained unaffected by the various kinds of criticism she was up against as a result of writing as what Mudrooroo terms a fringedweller "on the outskirts of the Metropolitan literary tradition of Europe" (20). Her position never was that of the silenced, fetished and thus controlled "other". But this, ironically enough, caused both her enormous popularity with her audience and her dismissal by the Aboriginalists.

Just as Aboriginalism has been a restrictive force in finding new ways of reading Aboriginal writings in English so has the atmosphere of liberal political correctness had unintentional hampering effects. When Oodgeroo stated that her poetry was "sloganistic, civil righterish, plain and simple" (Wright 13) critics generally gave up looking for formal aspects of her poetry that lay outside of accepted white standards of artistic expression and began to look at the contemporary political essence of Aboriginal identity found in her verse. The latter was a sensible effort altogether, except that such studies also suffered from the lack of effort to look behind the surface of the simple straightforward format of her words.[2]

Critics outside the school of Aboriginalism took to Oodgeroo — or perhaps in this instance Kath Walker — almost as a cherished national treasure or as their own symbol of redemption because her conciliatory poems gave them the chance to exorcise their own guilty feelings about a very racist Australia, and to indulge in the indisputable moral righteousness of Oodgeroo's plea to mankind. In Mudrooroo's words they turned "to the gentler Oodgeroo Noonuccal who accepts a common humanity" (148) rather than to the outrage and rancour of other writers such as Kevin Gilbert. Unfortunately, one might add, such studies, though compassionate and sympathetic to Oodgeroo's cause, never offered more than a superficial poet-in-her-own-right kind of reading of her poetry, and critics invariably came to present themselves as merely spokespersons for someone who was herself a spokesperson and therefore not in need of that.[3] Other critics have examined the strategies used to express Aboriginality in Oodgeroo's poems — though only at a rhetorical textual level (see, for instance, Chris Tiffin 1985) — and suggested that they range from defining Aboriginal people as victims, asking for sympathy, through an appeal to the common humanity of mankind: "We are the last of the Stone Age tribes,/Waiting for time to help us/As time helped you" (21), to a vision of a golden future without racial tensions: "when a juster justice/Grown wise and stronger/Points the bone no longer/At a darker race" (40). Other strategies are confrontation and the juxtaposition of contemporary oppression and past freedom as in "The Unhappy Race": "We want the old freedom and joy that all things have but you/Poor white man of the unhappy race" (19). The inevitable conclusion of such discussions, however, is that Oodgeroo's much-quoted melioristic outlook is at odds with a predominant stereotypical image of the Aboriginal person as sorrowful "last-of-the-tribe" victim who leads a rather one-dimensional life of being acted upon by the white man. The different voices of *My People* are seen as mere variations on the same mode of elegy. The ambivalence is not adequately addressed though, because marked swings and changes are seen as being beyond the poet's own control, as in the conclusion that "of all the correlatives to anger, meliorism is perhaps the saddest for it springs from an underlying hopelessness that it is trying to deny" (Beston 256).

Of course, Oodgeroo's poetry has to be seen as a product of its time and the 1960s — the period in which the poems of *My People* were all written — was a turbulent decade of political negotiation between Aboriginal and white Australians and indeed a period in which sentiments wavered between optimistic hope and angry disillusionment. The 1960s spelt the end of official paternalism, and important discussions about the differentiation between assimilation and integration took place. It should be remembered that Aboriginal people did not gain full citizen rights until 1967; prior to that citizenship was granted only to Aborigines who showed so-called good character and industrious habits and were keen to dissociate themselves from "native association" and assimilate into white Australian culture. In fact the kind of assimilation Oodgeroo fights against in her poetry — "Pour your pitcher of wine into the wide river/And where is your wine? There is only the river" (22) — was considered to be a policy which offered, and expected, Aboriginal people to take up the opportunity "to live as members of a single Australian community ... observing the same customs and influenced by the same beliefs, hopes and loyalties as other Australians" (Stevens 25-26). Even when in 1965 "same" was replaced by "similar" to promote the policy of integration, Australia was still thinking along basically monocultural lines, so the breakthrough of an Aboriginal voice into print was in itself an outstanding achievement.

There are numerous obvious explanations rooted in the Aboriginal world for the ambivalence found within that voice. While the form and the language Oodgeroo employed was standard European, the world from which she spoke was not. Oodgeroo was both observing that "in the Aboriginal world we give way to all emotions" (Turcotte 22) as well as embracing a polyphonic Aboriginal practice in which the artist functions as the custodian of the different voices of the people: "They dictate what I write ... I'm putting their voices on paper, writing their things" (Davidson 428-29). What Aboriginalists failed to observe in her verse was that the conflation of the authorial "I" and the collective "we" may indeed be a tribute paid to an ancient Aboriginal practice of storytelling: where one voice (story) ends another one takes over. Within this tradition — in which literature and politics in the broadest sense are not at all seen as antagonistic — individually is subjected to the concerns of the community. To look for a distinct personal voice as a marker of quality is a standard that has no validity in the Aboriginal tradition.

The majority of the poems in *My People* comprises voices that originate, however, in the peculiar fringe world, a third cultural reality midway between the traditional Aboriginal world and white society. This is in itself a highly ambivalent location in which, according to Mudrooroo, the Aboriginal writer is a "Janus-type figure" (24) who must fight for cultural space in an almost schizophrenic attempt to satisfy both Aboriginal and white audiences (125). The writer, he says:

> ... exists in ambiguity. White people assume that he or she is writing for the white world, the world of the invader. It is a curious fate — to write for a people not one's own, and stranger still to write for the conquerors of one's people. (148)

Since the fringe writer Oodgeroo had her own language stolen from her by white society she must both master the conqueror's standard language to get her message across and avoid the danger of "thinking white" while using it in an environment where every effort to assert an Aboriginal identity is circumscribed by white power. Such a tense and complex situation inevitably made her opt for writing in a double tongue as the best possible strategy to obtain what she considered the main objective of her art: equality.

Thus while the recurring shifts between ambiguity and assurance in Oodgeroo's poems may be seen as originating in the mood of the period in which they appeared as well as in the Aboriginal doctrine of community control, they are also the products of a deliberate fringe strategy that critics have tended to overlook because of the apparent transparency of Oodgeroo's verse. In that sense Oodgeroo as a poet was elusive and in fact safeguarding a strategic space of ambivalence. Her poems bargain; they linger between accommodating sentiments: "Let us try to understand the white man's ways/And accept them as they accept us" (2), in order not to make her white audience feel antagonistic towards her message, and a resistance that celebrates an exclusively Aboriginal spiritual affinity with the land: "Time to take a stand./Make the violent miner feel/Your violent/Love of land" (94). The recurring shift between seeing the past as "gone like our childhood days of old" (2) and "all about us and within" (93) is a similar tactical device of obliging white society while keeping the next well-prepared move in reserve.

It is, not surprisingly, again from the Aboriginal world itself

that guidelines to a much more complex understanding of
fringe writing — including Oodgeroo's poetry — come. Bruce
McGuinness has also commented on the particular position of
Aboriginal people existing in a dominant white world and how
that pertains to Aboriginal writing:

> They become actors in fact. They are able to act in numerous ways.
> They portray different images in different ways. With writing, we find
> that the same situation also occurs. When Aboriginal people write
> they write in a style. They're able to adopt various styles of writing
> so that what they really want to write about is there. It's hidden. It's
> contained within their writing, if one can go through the subterfuge,
> the camouflage that they use when they're writing. (47)

There is nothing simple and straightforward about a
communication situation that involves both Aboriginal people and
white Australians, as does indeed Oodgeroo's poetry, because there
is no equality between centre and fringe (Mudrooroo 153). Yet
Oodgeroo always retained her integrity by upholding what I see
as a strategic buffer zone between herself and the white world,
in which irrelevant criticism was lost upon her. This comes out
most strongly in interviews in which we find a clue to
understanding her tactics. When asked, for instance, how she
responded to the critics who thought she was a didactic writer of
propaganda she replies: "I agreed with them because it *was*
propaganda. I deliberately did it" — which completely defeats
the interviewer whose next question is almost rhetorical: "There
is no such thing as non-political writing, is there?". Oodgeroo's
answer, of course, is "That's right!" (Turcotte 19). Another
question concerns the two different voices speaking in her poetry:
"Gratefully we learn from you./The advanced race" (23) and
"Take care! White racists!/Blacks can be racist too./A violent
struggle could erupt/And racists meet their death" (89), and
whether one voice is truer than the other. Oodgeroo's answer is:
"No, I think they're on a par level. I think what you have to look
at is that I'm not talking about the humanitarians, I'm talking
about the real racists" (22), which leaves the interpretation of the
first bargaining voice in the air; deliberately of course. In another
interview Oodgeroo sets the rules of the game in a similar way.
The interviewer interrogates the curious fact that whereas a lot
of Oodgeroo's poems are about white oppression of Aboriginal

culture she turns around in poems like "Let Us Not Be Bitter" to argue that there are good whites who care. Oodgeroo replies: "Well isn't that true?" and hardly has the interviewer agreed before Oodgeroo is on to talk about just the opposite:

> ... we've learned all we could about the white man, how much have the whites learned about us? Are they slow learners? I'm coming to the conclusion that they must be ... In two hundred years wouldn't you have thought they have learned *something*? (Baker 290)

When Oodgeroo is not the least prepared to uncover the split between accommodation and resistance in her poetry, this may be due to the fact that she uses her poems to negotiate, by any means possible, a focus on how to remedy the problems from which Aboriginal people suffer under white hegemony. Plea and protest coexist because the former is used externally to attract the attention of socially-conscious white Australia — and to slightly disorientate members of the school of political correctness — whereas protest serves the function of mobilising the Aboriginal community internally.

The strategic discourses of the above-mentioned interviews suggest that despite the candid tone of Oodgeroo's verse we should expect what McGuinness terms subterfuge and camouflage to be at work in her poetry as well. Or we should recall Mudrooroo's advice to approach conventional fringe poetry written in standardised English "with a deeper sense of trying to read what may not be written, rather than what is written" (86). A reading of "United We Win" along those lines clearly illustrates that the poem bears more than a single meaning. The general tone — and the general reading — of the poem is one of forgiving reconciliation within the great Australian tradition of "mateship now and the good white hand stretched out to grip the black":

> The glare of a thousand years is shed on the black man's wistful face,
> Fringe-dweller now on the edge of towns, one of a dying race;
> But he has no bitterness in his heart for the white man just the same.

Inserted into this forced optimistic evaluation of the present and positive vision of the future, however, are the following lines:

> Curse no more the nation's great, the glorious pioneers,
> Murderers honoured with fame and wealth, won of our blood and tears;
> Brood no more on the bloody past that is gone without regret ... (79)

The bloody past, one feels and quite understands, is gone without regret *only* in as far as the poem anticipates the fulfilment of the vision. The second line of this quotation which identifies the pioneers of European Australia as murderers, however, stands out discordantly as anything but forgiving. It is almost like an Aboriginal "Lest We Forget" that contains complex references and deeper layers of communication than the surface context of absolution implies. There is a silence of blood and tears behind that subterfuge that suddenly begins to speak of what is not written in the poem: the fictitious story of "terra nullius" and the blanket of forgetfulness thrown over the near genocide of the First Australians which is the real legacy of White Australia. This camouflaged story — in a double sense — is set off against the proclaimed legacy of the Australian nation by Oodgeroo's re-use of the ballad form (even if it is not an ironic re-use) associated with Lawson and the socialist stance of the Australian democratic tradition. The unwritten text then is rather less accommodating than the written one as it presents both Lawson — who, seen with Aboriginal eyes, was racist — as well as the grand bushman tradition as ignoble, because besides not inviting Aboriginal people into the fraternity it simply wrote them out of existence and into silence. Yet that is the very silence that speaks of exclusiveness from behind lines which celebrate possible unity. Thus, behind the strategically outstretched hand there always seems to be the impatient fist. These two images are much like two schemes that intersect in the political moment when the white audience, taking up the plea, reflect on their own collective guilt and turn it into more fruitful action while simultaneously Aboriginal people come together to set out the conditions on which they want to live as equal "fellow Australians". In Oodgeroo's re-use of the nursery rhyme we find a similar redirection of a standard form (see Indyk 254-55), most effectively, however, in the poem "No More Boomerang" in which quite severe criticism of the destructive influences of so-called civilisation is located behind the subterfuge of humour (according to Oodgeroo an Aboriginal survival strategy of vital importance). The form itself evokes memories of childhood and innocence, a simple literary form with a socialising impulse. In the Aboriginal context, however, there is an ironic and political twist to the use of the form, because paternalism was in fact still

a strong influence on white perceptions of Aboriginal people at
the time when the poem was written; the idea that they were
children of civilisation and needed enlightenment had not yet faded
away. In the disguised naivety characteristic of the form, the poem
revolves around the losses and gains of Aboriginal people since
the coming of European civilisation:

> No more boomerang
> No more spear;
> Now all civilised —
> Colour bar and beer.
>
> . . . .
>
> No more sharing
> What the hunter brings.
> Now we work for money,
> Then pay it back for things.
>
> . . . .
>
> No more firesticks
> That made the whites scoff.
> Now all electric,
> And no better off.
>
> . . . .
>
> No more message-stick;
> Lubras and lads
> Got television now,
> Mostly ads.

Yet ends with the rhyme of political punch:

> Lay down the woomera,
> Lay down the waddy.
> Now we got atom-bomb,
> End *every*body. (33)

There is a very direct text behind the simple humorous facade here
by a mature, superior Aboriginal commenting on an infantile,
misguided white race; a text which possibly could not be written
at the time in overt political terms. However, it has many echoes
of Oodgeroo in interview: ''White Australians have got a lot to
learn. I hope we will be tolerant enough to teach them'' (Turcotte
27). For Aboriginal people there is no salvation to be found in
waiting for time and ''civilisation'' to help them (21). On the

contrary, the only salvation is the offer to become indigenised which is presented to White Australia beneath the lines of ''No More Boomerang''.

As it has appeared from this discussion, Oodgeroo's approach to poetics is not experimental but rather governed by political expediency and the still unresolved conflict between the colonisers and the colonised in Australia. We find in her verse no abrogation of the English language, no distinct appropriations or subversive rewritings of the coloniser's forms, but her poems are a far cry from being just a gentle derivation of the European poetic tradition. The tension that exists between her various poems in terms of both form and content derives in fact from the tension between the white world she addresses and the fringe world she represents, and produces within and between her poems a strategic space that is functional and highly political. Sometimes the voice speaking from that space is unreserved and forthright: ''Do not ask us/To be deserters, to disown our mother/To change the unchangeable./The gum cannot be trained into an oak/'' (22); and at other times it is arranged as political manoeuvre: ''With new knowledge, a new world opened./Suddenly caught up in the white man's ways/Gladly and gratefully we accept,/And this is necessity'' (84); an acceptance in the guise of reverence to make the white man ''Give the deal you still deny us'' (36)[4]. While it may be argued from a 1990s perspective that ''there will always be some suspicion that the forms, or at least the values implicit in them, could prove more powerful than the . . . intention which governs their use'' (Indyk 249), Oodgeroo's poetry was extremely influential as the platform from which Aboriginal poetry has since moved onwards (in the poetry of, for instance, Mudrooroo and Lionel Fogarty). If Oodgeroo gave a voice to Aboriginal silences Aboriginal poets have now turned that into a separate poetic language — and as a political statement of a time when no real authenticity was granted to the fringe dweller's world. Her words rushed into print at just the right time. Oodgeroo was the first Aboriginal poet to be published in English and, says Kevin Gilbert in *Inside Black Australia*: ''Her intensive efforts to gain social and political change have never wavered'':

hers was [then] virtually a voice in the wilderness and was, without a doubt, a major contributing factor in the recognition of citizenship rights for Aboriginals following the . . . 1967 Referendum.'' (94)

What grander impact can be imaged for Oodgeroo's work? More than anything Oodgeroo's art was an important political act — never art for art's sake, which is why her poetry is not adaptable to criticism for the sake of criticism, and cannot readily be contained within the latest academic trends in which the critics themselves tend to become the centre of concern. Oodgeroo was very much an Aboriginal song-maker charting maps of the fringe dwellers' lives. She never divorced herself from her community but remained the caretaker of her people's very important political stories. She was a freedom fighter who wedded her life to the recovery and the advancement of her people. Even when writing black words on a white page she was drawing charred sticks across the paperbark at the same time. She was, as it were, the devoted and resilient Oodgeroo of her own legend who envisioned a plan, a strategy and a goal.

WORKS CITED

Anonymous. "Review." *Australian Book Review* May 1964.

Baker, Candida. *Yacker 2: Australian Writers Talk About Their Work.* Sydney: Pan Books, 1987.

Beston, John. "The Aboriginal Poets in English: Kath Walker, Jack Davis and Kevin Gilbert." *Meanjin* 36.4 (1977): 446-61.

Cantrell, Leon. "Review." *Poetry Magazine* (1967).

Davidson, Jim. "Interview: Kath Walker". *Meanjin* 36.4 (1977): 428-41.

Gilbert, Kevin. *Inside Black Australia: An Anthology of Aboriginal Poetry.* Ringwood: Penguin, 1988.

Hodge, Bob, and Vijay Mishira. *Dark Side of the Dream: Australian Literature and the Postcolonial Mind.* North Sydney: Allen and Unwin, 1991.

Indyk, Ivor. "Assimilation or Appropriation: Uses of European Literary Forms in Black Australian Writing." *Australian Literary Studies* 15.4 (1992): 249-60.

McGuinness, Bruce, and Denis Walker. "The Politics of Aboriginal Literature." *Aboriginal Writing Today.* Ed. Jack Davis and Bob Hodge. Canberra: AIAS, 1985.

Noonuccal, Oodgeroo. "Paperbark." *Aboriginal Culture Today.* Ed. Anna Rutherford. Sydney: Dangaroo P, 1988.

_____ (as Kath Walker). *My People.* 2nd ed. Milton: Jacaranda P, 1981

Mudrooroo (as Mudrooroo Narogin). *Writing from the Fringe: A Study of Modern Aboriginal Literature.* Melbourne: Hyland House, 1990.

Stevens, Frank. *Black Australia.* Sydney: Aura P, 1981.

Tiffin, Chris. "Look to the New-Found Dreaming: Identity and Technique in Australian Aboriginal Writing." *Journal of Commonwealth Literature* 20.1 (1985): 156-70.

Turcotte, Gerry. "Recording the Cries of the People — An Interview tih Oodgeroo (Kath Walker)." *Aboriginal Culture Today*. Ed. Anna Rutherford. Sydney: Dangaroo P, 1988.

Wright, Judith. "A New Literature: The Voice of the Australian Aboriginals." *Solidarity* 9.5 (1975).

NOTES

1   In addition to poems written between 1966 and 1970, the volume contains poems from both *We Are Going* (1964) and *The Dawn Is at Hand* (1966).

2   A notable exception is Adam Shoemaker's *Black Words White Page: Aboriginal Literature 1929-1988* (St Lucia: U of Queensland P, 1989).

3   As Chris Tiffin notes the "poet in her own right" label locates Aboriginal writers "in a tradition of white writing, yet we are reminded the authors are novices in this tradition whereas we are the experienced readers" (158).

4   This is similar to Oodgeroo's response to the question whether or not Aboriginal people should accept 1988-Bicentennial grants — "blood money": "I answer we've been picking up blood money for two hundred years ... I say pick it up and run with it and use it against them. I'm all for it" (Turcotte 28-29).

Voices:
Educationist, Activist,
Performer

Oodgeroo — an Educator Who Proved One Person Could Make a Difference

Rhonda Craven

Introduction

For those of us who knew Oodgeroo well and loved her dearly our attempts to contribute to this book are difficult as we are still mourning her. I have been told to tell it like it is and to provide details of the hard-hitting edge of Oodgeroo's role as an educator. Despite being an academic I will write my contribution to this book in the style of Oodgeroo's people — that of oral history — as a tribute to Oodgeroo, her family, her friends and her people. Hence I am deliberately going to state the story I have to tell from my own personal perspective to reach out to all Australians who loved her.

I would like to thank Oodgeroo's sister Aunty Lucy for spending some time with me. I have been rather reluctant to start to write this as it is something that engages me in grieving a great loss to my own personal life. Aunty Lucy has motivated me to write down what I know just by saying she is looking forward to reading this book to see what people who really loved Oodgeroo have to say. I will do my best to do justice to your wish. I also believe judging from the reports in the papers that not many people seem to know about the work Oodgeroo was doing in the final years of her life and how this work will lay the foundation for positive social change in this country through education. The legacy of Oodgeroo's work and her recorded words contain the key elements of the directions Australia as a country needs in order to reconcile non-Aboriginal Australians with Aboriginal Australians.

Oodgeroo — the Educator

Oodgeroo proved that one person could make a difference. Her life was dedicated to a cause. Many times she spoke to me about this — of the importance of the struggle over her personal life and her beliefs in her destiny being to a higher calling — a calling for humanity. Oodgeroo's poem "My Love" (*My People*, 3rd ed. 46) clearly documents her feelings on this.

> The social part, the personal
>   I have renounced of old;
> Mine is a dedicated life,
>   No man's to have and hold.

I, like many other people, also know of the enormous sacrifices she made in her own personal life to achieve this goal. Repeatedly Oodgeroo has told me her own children have grown up "behind her back".

> It is something I wouldn't want anyone else to go through because they grew up behind my back. I was looking after the tribe. You see in the Aboriginal world the protocol ... is you think first of your tribe; the individual comes last on the list. So you see the Aboriginal tribe took precedence over the children because I was upholding the law of the Aborigine. (*Oodgeroo Noonuccal — A Life*)

This by no means infers that Oodgeroo was saying that she neglected her kids; it is testimony though to the enormous personal sacrifices she has made to get a better deal for her people.

Oodgeroo's life was not dedicated to the arts, rather she utilised every skill she had to educate. "Education held the key to logical race relations but Australia's system was in urgent need of an overhaul," she said (*Griffith Gazette* 1989: 7). Time after time I asked Oodgeroo how she wanted to be described in programs and always she insisted her role as an Educator be listed first. This wasn't some sort of hype to promote herself as a teacher with many doctorates to her name; it was what she was on about — the fundamental importance of education as being the key to the struggle for Aboriginal rights in Australia. "There is no doubt that education, correctly applied, can meet our future needs" (*Griffith Gazette* 7). This meant that she called on all her varied talents to achieve this aim.

> My first book *We Are Going*: they said it was a very bitter book. I didn't see it that way. It was hard-hitting and then they said it was propaganda — which I bowed to ... and said yes it is. It's the only

way I can educate — public propaganda. I'm prepared to do it. I'll
do anything to get a message across. (*Dean's Inaugural Lecture*)

It also meant that she educated both black and white Australians.
In fact, Oodgeroo initiated the process of reconciliation long before
governments seriously considered the concept and way, before it
became "fashionable". Oodgeroo set out to make a bridge
between two different worlds and the tool she used to do this was
education.

> I wanted to explain to the children both black and white the meaning
> of *terra nullius* ... Aboriginals have been so badly treated by the
> European invaders some of them really hated them for what they did
> and I'm trying to say, "don't hate them — educate them". Teach
> them — teach them the truth about it so they can be our allies ...
> I think that when we've told the white Australian people about it,
> that they will understand it and we'll get a lot of friends helping us
> to get what we need in order to act as free people in this country.
> (Noonuccal, *Film Interview*).

Oodgeroo's message was always delivered powerfully and she knew
how to use her position to influence education systems.

> European Australians must let go of England. American universities
> are the leaders in providing cultural role models for students. We must
> duplicate that pattern or must I as an Aboriginal Elder, advise
> Aboriginal students to seek higher education in America? (*Griffith
> Gazette* 7).

She wasn't shy about saying what she thought; for example, she
described the bicentenary as "two hundred years of sheer,
unadulterated humiliation". Nor did she try and force young
people to adopt her view, feeling instead that:

> All you can do is give the young the benefit of your experience. I'm
> not going to dictate to them what they should be doing. That's their
> responsibility, not mine. I just want to be able to look myself fair
> in the eye and say, win lose or draw, I've done my best. (Qtd.
> Wooldridge 1046)

For her own people she ensured their voice was heard and
supported. She encouraged all indigenous Australians to continue
to lift their voices and, whether they be young people, Elders or
Aboriginal prisoners, to take pride in their Aboriginality and to

stand up and change a system that openly sought to discriminate against them. Oodgeroo was a ''constant reminder to the wider community of the pride and spirituality of indigenous Australians. Australia will always be indebted to her for the depth of appreciation of this land that she sought to make available for all to share'' (Dodson 1043). She was a trail blazer in that she attacked the heart of white Australia and called upon all decent non-Aboriginal Australians to join the struggle. Many, to their credit, did and still are supporting Aboriginal people. Her words were designed to educate and their influence spread to many other shores around this planet. One only has to see and try to reply to overseas mail both before and after her death to know how pervasive her influence as an educator has been.

Oodgeroo and I

I met Oodgeroo only recently, compared to many of her friends. However, I have the privilege of not just knowing Oodgeroo but of sharing a unique and special relationship with her, a relationship that developed only over a four-year period. The relationship that we had and still have after her passing is that I have the honour of being — in Oodgeroo's words, and in my heart — ''the daughter she never had''. What is unique, I suppose, about this is that I am non-Aboriginal and at the time of meeting Oodgeroo less than half her age — Oodgeroo's heart had no notion of racism. Oodgeroo also had special relationships with other young Australians and some of these people include: Lydia Miller, Rhoda Roberts and Annie Hanlon. Oodgeroo could foresee the importance of educating young Aboriginal and non-Aboriginal Australians as she wanted to ensure young people continued the work she began.

Over the period I have known Oodgeroo I have learnt that education is not about what you know but rather about looking at yourself as a person before you begin. I thought she had come to teach me how to teach Aboriginal Studies. What I didn't know at the time was that this would involve Oodgeroo's teaching me about life itself and scrutinising my own life. Oodgeroo often said to me, ''I will make you or break you, but I hope to make you.'' She also said that she must have done something really bad for the Earth Mother to make her get stuck with me.

Oodgeroo — the latter years

I first met Oodgeroo in 1990 when she delivered the inaugural Dean's lecture at the University of New South Wales, St George Campus. Here, like elsewhere around Australia, she packed the theatre and kept staff and students enthralled. After her lecture I was asked to take her to meet with an Aboriginal community from Western Sydney — the Darug people. This was the beginning of Oodgeroo's special relationship with the Darug. The Darug have very few surviving Elders so Oodgeroo took it upon herself to meet frequently with members of the Darug community over her last years, teaching them Noonuccal arts and crafts and supporting them with her guidance when it was sought. Oodgeroo understood the importance of strengthening and supporting individual Aboriginal communities across the country. Hence her role as an educator was extended to communities as well as individuals and organisations.

Oodgeroo returned to the university for a period of four months in 1991 as a UNSW Literary Fellow. During this period Oodgeroo not only asked to teach UNSW students across all faculties but particularly requested that a significant period of time be spent at St George Campus, so that she could concentrate on teaching our student teachers. As any one page of her diary of this period will show she did not confine her fellowship to the bounds of the university but freely gave her time to other universities, schools, Aboriginal organisations and Koori prisoners in between the usual numerous requests for interviews with the media.

When Oodgeroo visited Sylvania Public School in 1992, she was asked to dedicate a big, old gum tree. "Don't do gum trees," she said spiritedly. "Only do paperbarks." So she dedicated a paperbark tree (a melaleuca) to the Tharawal community of the area. She pleased everybody but herself as she saw each invitation as a chance to educate more people. In fact, as her secretary over this period I found it difficult to schedule all the things she wanted to do in her diary and found that while my energy levels were waning hers were still well-primed. After Oodgeroo had taught some 30 000 children about her culture at her home "Moongalba" on North Stradbroke Island, the demands of Sydney life were to her minimal.

It was at this time that she called for all Australians to be taught

Aboriginal Studies in schools and received a letter of support from Minister Robert Tickner. At this time she also launched her own campaign to support the Mabo case. The theme of the campaign was summarised on a poster, devised and reproduced with Oodgeroo's own money. The poster features three simple words with a powerful message: "Don't Hate — Educate", followed by the phrase "Time to terminate *Terra Nullius* — the lie". She launched this campaign with a keynote address at the inaugural Aboriginal Studies Association Conference and called upon Australians "to burn the present English Constitution and replace it with an Australian Constitution which meets the needs of all races now living in Australia". She stated "Time for a more enlightened approach. Time for a change for the better. Time to outlaw racism in Australia. Time to rectify *Terra Nullius* — The Lie" (Noonuccal & Walker 92). The tool she perceived as the key to this process was education.

During 1991 Oodgeroo decided that the only way education was going to help to make a more just society for all Australians was by ensuring children were taught the truth about the real history of this country. She believed children are our nation's future. She said:

> Children are not born racists; they have to be taught it. They are born free of any of those silly attitudes and it's not until they are taught to be a racist they become a racist. (*Film Interview*)

> Change will come. The little ones today will be the adults of tomorrow and change will come when we get them talking to each other — the Aboriginal children and all minority groups — whatever race they are in this country; when they start talking to one another then, and only then, can Australians call themselves a multicultural society. At the present time all we've got is a multicultural people — we have yet to build a society. And, furthermore, for the information of the unenlightened — the Aboriginals of Australia were a multicultural society long before the invasion. (*The First Born*)

She then instigated what may become her most significant contribution to Australian society — a proposal to design a mandatory model for an Aboriginal Studies subject for student primary teachers. She perceived teaching the teachers as the only way to ensure that reconciliation would occur. Despite the fact that universities had failed to see the need for this approach in the teacher education curriculum and that the wall of silence about Aboriginal history and society was firmly in place in most teacher education institutions across the country in 1991, Oodgeroo dared to dream the impossible and, in so doing, challenge the conscience of academic White Australia.

> Last year I was awarded a fellowship at the University of New South Wales. I accepted gladly as I had a dream. A Dream of uniting the best of all races now living in this beautiful country that we the Aboriginals inherited from our Earth Mother the Rainbow Serpent ... Let us unite with the best of all races so we can create a better living for all. Let the Dream which is your dream as well as mine become a reality so that we can escape by walking away from the nightmare of the last 200 years. (*Beyond Terra Nullius*)

Her goal was simple: to teach the teacher educators how to teach student teachers so that the teachers could educate all Australians about our country's history and that of indigenous peoples — the ultimate reconciliation strategy.

She approached the then Dean of the Faculty of Professional Studies, Professor Tony Vinson, and asked him if the university would support and co-ordinate this initiative and ensure it became a reality. At this time she also negotiated with the Dean for three years of my life to be devoted to coordinating this project on her behalf. Professor Vinson promptly responded to Oodgeroo's request by writing a letter to Minister Robert Tickner to request funding, and the Minister agreed to give the university a seeding grant of $20 000 to explore how such a project could be developed. Reflecting on this, Robert Tickner acknowledged that Oodgeroo ''was also committed to seeing that, most importantly, teachers learnt as part of their regular training to teach Aboriginal history and culture effectively, and advanced that objective through her own involvement in a very important recent initiative of the University of New South Wales'' (Tickner 1046).

Oodgeroo began to establish a New South Wales-based Steering Committee. She sought the assistance of New South Wales Aboriginal Education Consultative Group Incorporated (NSW AECG Inc.) in collaborating with her as Joint Principal Consultants to develop the consultative mechanisms that could ensure such a project was a success. At this time I was worried sick about whether the project would attract the support of

Aboriginal educators whose support and direction was essential to ensure indigenous people could determine the structure and content of such a subject. Oodgeroo on the other hand held a quietly confident attitude and was forever saying "There is no need to stress out. My people will come."

And come they did — from schools, education authorities, Aboriginal organisations and communities — Elders, young teachers, members of professional associations and leading Aboriginal educators. Not just enough people to form a Steering Committee but enough people to form a vast consultative network that stretched across the nation. Thousands of Australians both black and white, all with one goal in mind: to support in whatever way they could the teaching of teachers about Aboriginal history and culture. The consultation generated is seen by NSW AECG Inc. as one of the most thorough consultative processes undertaken in Aboriginal Education. It is a process that is still attracting Australians to assist in 1994.

The project is designed to develop model tertiary teaching resources that include sample lecture/tutorial notes, a student teacher-oriented reference resource, model sample teaching activities and teacher-oriented videotapes. Oodgeroo has played a key role in developing these materials with the Steering Committee. The subject is designed in such a way that other universities can adapt the materials to meet the needs of their local Aboriginal communities and, in fact, in no two institutions will the subject be taught in the same way. It is a tribute to Oodgeroo that over the period 1991-1994 there are now seven universities in Australia trialling a core Aboriginal Studies subject when previously there was only one. It also proves that indeed one person can make a difference.

In 1993, when the Commonwealth formally handed over project funding to the University, Oodgeroo told Minister Tickner that she hoped to live to see all primary school teachers having to take a mandatory Aboriginal Studies subject as part of their teacher education course. It was her last wish that this project succeed. She saw this project as emphasising reconciliation through education. When Oodgeroo was very ill she assured me that the project would succeed in that she had laid the pathway for its success. In a life full of monumental contributions to Australian society her last project may prove to be her most significant for generations of Australians to come. Oodgeroo's achievements in her latter years are testimony that "at the time she died she was still active on the great issues confronting Australia" (Holding 1050).

Summary

Australia has lost a living national treasure but Oodgeroo's work will live on in the hearts and minds of her people, in the hearts and minds of educators, and in the hearts and minds of all Australians. Oodgeroo has given all Australians a special legacy. She has opened the pathway for all Australians to walk together and create a better future for all. Oodgeroo believed education was the key. By opening the hearts and minds of Australians to our true history and by providing educational strategies for social justice, Oodgeroo has set the scene for harmony and respect of different cultures in Australia's multicultural society.

For those of you who loved Oodgeroo, her message is not to mourn her passing but to celebrate her life. As Denis, Oodgeroo's son, said at her funeral, "the main message is reconciliation healing and peace, and the only way we are going to get that is through mutual respect — mutual respect for our culture and all other cultures". In death she was as unselfish as she was in life. It is now up to us to tread the pathways set by Oodgeroo and walk together side by side to make a better Australia based on mutual respect and understanding. As James Miller, Koori author and teacher educator, says: "Australia is far better than it once was for Aboriginal people but not as good as it might become." Oodgeroo's legacy to all who loved her is the understanding that we can help to make a better Australia a reality and to prove to all Australians that one person can make a difference.

WORKS CITED

Dodson, Pat. *Condolences, Current House Hansard*. 27 September 1993: 1043.

Holding, Clive. *Condolences, Current House Hansard*. 27 September 1993: 1050.

Noonuccal, Oodgeroo. *Griffith Gazette*. Griffith University, 10 May 1989: 7.

———. *My People*. 3rd ed. Milton: Jacaranda P, 1990.

———. *Dean's Inaugural Lecture*. University of New South Wales, St George Campus, 1991.

_____ . *Film Interview at the Second Annual Aboriginal Studies Association Conference*. University of New South Wales, Kensington Campus, 1992.

_____ . *Beyond Terra Nullius — the Lie*. Videotape of Keynote address 2nd Annual Aboriginal Studies Association Conference. University of New South Wales, Kensington Campus, 1992.

_____ . Quoted in *Oodgeroo Noonuccal — A Life*. ABC film documentary, 1993.

_____ . Quoted in *The First Born*. Audio-Cassette produced by QANTAS, 1993.

_____ , and Denis Walker. *Aboriginal Studies in the 90s: Where to Now?* Ed. R.G. Craven and N. Parbury. Collected papers of the inaugural ASA Conference, University of New South Wales, October 1991. 88-92.

Miller, James. *Why Teach Aboriginal Studies?* Film produced by the University of New South Wales Steering Committee Australian Indigenous Studies for Teacher Education Courses.

Tickner, Robert. *Condolences, Current House Hansard*. 27 September 1993: 1045.

Wooldridge, M. *Condolences, Current House Hansard*. 27 September 1993: 1046.

Oodgeroo: A Pioneer in Aboriginal Education

Alan Duncan

"White people want to do something about Aborigines, but they don't know how to go about it," said Kath Walker (Oodgeroo) to reporter Jim Hall of the *Sun Herald* in June 1964. Hall was reporting on the phenomenal success of Kath's first book of poems, *We Are Going*, which had sold out two editions within a few days of reaching the bookshops.

Hall described the Aboriginal author as "A poem scribbler from childhood who never took her poems seriously until she joined the Federal Council for Aboriginal Advancement of which she is Queensland Branch Secretary". This link between Kath's writings and her involvement in the Aboriginal rights movement has often been overlooked by students of her poetry. It is not possible, however, to overlook the very close relationship between Kath Walker's fight for Aboriginal rights and her work as an educator. Indeed, throughout the 1960s, the whole "raison d'être" for her work in education was her passion for justice for Aborigines.

At a Saturday evening function at the 1962 Annual Conference of FCAATSI held in Adelaide, Kath presented her "Aboriginal Charter of Rights" with folk singer Gary Shearston — who had set the poem to music. Its powerful educational message was fully appreciated by all of the delegates present. The "Charter" and a number of the other poems which appeared in Kath's first book were honed in the Aboriginal rights movement.

Throughout the 1960s Kath Walker accepted her major role as an educator as she became increasingly involved in the campaign to have the Australian constitution amended. Her primary targets were federal members of parliament. Kath had a close ally in Gordon Bryant, the federal member for Wills and the senior vice-president of FCAATSI. Through Bryant, she began to lobby members from both sides of the political spectrum and led, or participated in, many deputations.

On one occasion, on a deputation to Sir Robert Menzies, Kath was offered a drink by the ever-hospitable Prime Minister. With a twinkle in her eyes, she drew the PM's attention to the fact that in Queensland where she lived, legislation provided for a heavy fine or even a jail sentence for any white person "providing spirituous liquor to an Aborigine". Menzies was rather taken aback. While he quickly made the rejoinder that "I am the boss around here", he realised that the remark was part of the campaign to have the Federal Government accept responsibility for Aboriginal affairs, or at least to have the question put to the Australian people by way of a referendum. At the 1963 Annual Conference of FCAATSI Kath Walker was one of the 25 Aborigines among the 100 or more delegates who attended. She spoke strongly in favour of a four-part motion from the Education Committee which called for:

> 1. All State Education Departments to appoint a suitably qualified officer to investigate the requirements and establish special education facilities including preschool, technical and adult education for Aborigines.
> 2. All State Education Departments to accept responsibility for Aborigines with fully trained teachers.
> 3. Teacher Unions in all States to conduct a survey on conditions in Aboriginal schools.
> 4. The Commonwealth Government to conduct a survey of the real educational needs of tribal Aborigines and the preservation of their culture.[1]

It was these four principles which Kath adopted in her approach to the need for reform in Aboriginal education but she also spoke strongly in support of other policies adopted by FCAATSI on such matters as health, housing, employment, equal wages and social conditions. Unlike some of her contemporaries, Kath always emphasised the positive side of the campaign and the need for both races to work together. Her quick wit and high intelligence were demonstrated time and time again.

In her major role as an educator in the referendum campaign, Kath Walker not only spoke at rallies organised by FCAATSI and its state bodies but also spoke at service clubs and at schools where her audience had to be convinced of the rightness of the Aboriginal cause. During the 1960s there were few Aborigines who had had the educational opportunities to equip them for public speaking and many others who were too shy or too afraid to speak out or challenge the establishment. Kath faced a particularly difficult time in Queensland, which had a very poor record in terms of concern for the Aboriginal population.

Despite Kath's growing reputation as a poet with national and international recognition, there were many in her own state who joined in the smear campaign against her and others in the Aboriginal rights movement who were attempting to awaken the conscience of her contemporaries. In Brisbane, the major Aboriginal organisation recognised by the authorities was OPAL (One People for Australia League) which included many leading citizens who supported an improvement in Aboriginal conditions, but mainly through their assimilation into the wider community.

A major Aboriginal spokesperson for OPAL was Neville (later Senator) Bonner. It was a mark of Kath's integrity that she never attempted to confront or personally denigrate her rival but spoke more in sorrow than in anger as she quietly continued her campaign to educate the community on the way it should approach the question of Aboriginal advancement. As well as her education campaign in Queensland, Kath often visited Sydney where she was involved in the Aboriginal Adult Education program conducted by the Department of Adult Education at the University of Sydney.

In 1963, the NSW Aborigines' Welfare Board and the Education Department agreed to appoint me to initiate programs in Aboriginal adult education at Sydney University, as I had been a principal in both Aboriginal and mixed-race schools. It was assumed that I would start literacy classes for adult Aborigines; but using the academic freedom provided by my university appointment, I initiated projects in Community Development and Leadership Training in Aboriginal communities.

It is possible that I may have been influenced to adopt this type of approach by the fact that I was on the executive of FCAATSI. One of my closest allies was Kath Walker, who relished the opportunity to work in a constructive way with Aborigines. Although Kath worked in a voluntary capacity as a trainer she claimed she was a learner and student and soaked up information, especially on Aboriginal culture, from all others involved in the project.

There can be no doubt that Kath was a born teacher. She was well aware that many adult Aborigines had little in the way of educational attainments but that this was entirely due to a lack of opportunity rather than to any lack of innate ability. She realised that the most urgent need was to build up self-confidence in the students whose self-concepts had been so severely damaged by their previous educational experiences.

At one of the early leadership training courses in 1964, an arrangement had been made with one of the local Chambers of Commerce for the Aboriginal participants to be involved in their first formal debate. The agreed topic was that "Assimilation Is in the Best Interests of Aboriginal People" and it was also agreed that the Aboriginal leaders could choose to take the government or the opposition side. Despite a lot of encouragement from both Kath and myself, none of the other participants in the Leadership School except Pastor Doug Nicholls (later Sir Douglas, Governor of South Australia) could be cajoled into representing the university team.

As the leader and first speaker, Kath's performance could only be described as brilliant. Her team almost faced disaster, however, when Pastor Doug interjected during the debate with the remark "You can't say that!" when one of the Chamber's speakers stated that "Aborigines had no future unless they became like whites". Kath gave Doug a jab in the ribs which almost took his breath away. In her summation at the end of the debate, she pointed out that Doug had never previously seen, let alone been involved in, a formal debate of any kind and was simply demonstrating traditional Aboriginal honesty which could well be destroyed if he was forced to adopt the white man's laws — which demanded that no interjections be made during a formal debate. She spoke with such conviction that the adjudicator had no alternative but to award the debate to the Aboriginal team.

It was Kath's work after the debate, however, which was so valuable. She carefully explained to the other Aboriginal participants in the leadership school how important it was for them to be involved in such an exercise so they could prove, beyond reasonable doubt, that Aborigines could use white customs and rules and demonstrate their undoubted superiority without sacrificing their dignity. Using her educational skills to the fullest extent, she concentrated on the affective rather than on the cognitive aspects of learning and naturally achieved a great deal of success. The rise in self-esteem and self-worth among the other Leadership School participants was quite palpable. Kath used every opportunity she could find to enhance the concept and feelings of self-confidence among Aborigines since she was well aware of the vital importance of this aspect of learning.

It should be noted that Kath's involvement in the Leadership Training Schools was purely on a voluntary basis, as it was with all other participants. During the 1960s and early '70s neither the government nor the university was prepared to make any contribution towards the cost of the leadership schools. Indeed the ideas of leadership training and community development for the Aboriginal population was not viewed favourably in official circles. The program depended on small donations from voluntary organisations and on the assistance of such people as Kath Walker, whose fares were provided by her publisher when she was required to visit Sydney on official business.

Much of my own work was considered as suspect or even dangerous in promoting Aboriginal rights during the period when anti-Communism was rampant and when all protest movements were erroneously considered to be the work of communist agitators. Although my salary was met by the university, financial support for the programs was very minimal.

Every Easter from 1963, Kath would travel to Canberra for the annual FCAATSI Conference and she took the opportunity to educate the growing number of Aboriginal delegates — especially the younger ones such as Gary Foley and Ken Brindle — of the importance of developing and maintaining a sense of pride in the rich cultural heritage of all Aboriginal people. She also urged them to accept an increased degree of responsibility for their own advancement and not to spend all their time on negative criticism of whites for the lack of progress. She also stressed that it was educational opportunities and not dependence on welfare handouts which was required to improve the Aboriginal situation. As the Secretary of the Queensland Council of Aborigines and Torres

Strait Islanders (later the Aboriginal Rights Council) Kath was always busy, not only with a heavy round of speaking engagements to the general community but also in working with and educating her Aboriginal contemporaries.

At the 1965 Easter Conference of FCAATSI it was decided to launch a public campaign of deputations, letters and telegrams to all federal members of parliament urging a referendum on increasing federal responsibilities for Aborigines. When, in 1967, the Commonwealth Government finally acquiesced to increasing public demand for the referendum, it was Kath Walker who became the Chairperson of the "Vote Yes" Committee in Queensland — and her educational work began in earnest.

At the referendum the Australian people were asked to support or reject two proposals to change the Australian constitution. These changes were to delete Section 127 and to delete the proviso at the end of Section 51 (xxxvi) which excluded Aborigines from special legislation by the Commonwealth Parliament. The relevant sections read:

> Section 127 In reckoning the numbers of the people of the Commonwealth or of a State, or other part of the Commonwealth, Aboriginal natives shall not be counted.

> Section 51 The Parliament shall, subject to the Constitution, have powers to make laws for the order and good government of the Commonwealth with respect to: the people of any race, other than the Aboriginal race in any State, for whom it is deemed necessary to make special laws.[2]

While the "Vote Yes" Committee in each state felt fairly confident that the repeal of Section 127 would be supported, they knew that there was some resistance to the assumption of commonwealth powers in respect of Aborigines. Kath Walker threw herself wholeheartedly into the campaign, realising that Queensland was one of the states with the most repressive legislation against Aborigines and that the Aborigines in her state had a lot to gain. She spoke at meetings organised by churches, trade unions, service clubs, voluntary organisations, to the press and to anyone she thought would be of assistance. During the campaign the magazines of most churches and trade union bodies gave strong support to the "Vote Yes" campaign.

At a conference of the Anthropology Society at the University of Queensland Kath told the gathering of academics that, because of discrimination and apathy. Aborigines had advanced only as far as the Australian rubbish dumps and reserves. Her work was not without cost, however, as she wrote in an autobiographical note included in the book *Turning the Tide*, a personal history of FCAATSI by Faith Bandler. Kath wrote that soon after she returned from a tour of other states when she averaged from seven to ten interviews a day for the media, she attended a local meeting one night, but on her return home "found that someone had entered my house and savagely slashed the curtains and all my clothes with a razor. I was very shocked and my companions phoned the police several times but they didn't come" (Bandler 155).

During this period, the Australian Security and Intelligence Organisation (ASIO) attended many public meetings organised by FCAATSI or local state Aboriginal organisations where they took notes and photographs. It was also believed that the phones of most executive members were tapped as the referendum campaign coincided with the Vietnam protest movement and the security service apparently felt that the claims for Aboriginal rights posed a threat to the Australian nation. Despite the long record of rejection of nearly all previous constitutional referenda, the campaign on the Aboriginal questions was an outstanding success. It is significant that the result in Queensland — where an 89.21% "Yes vote" was achieved — was better than that obtained in both Western Australia and South Australia. The educational strategies orchestrated by Kath, with the assistance of her many colleagues, had achieved a remarkable victory.

Now that Aborigines were officially included in the national census, one of the early tasks of the Commonwealth Government was to establish a definition of an Aborigine which could be applied throughout the continent. In a number of deputations and submissions to parliamentarians, Kath and her colleagues had pointed out the absurdity of having a different definition of an Australian Aborigine for each state and territory. For example, in Western Australia people of less than one-quarter Aboriginal descent were not classified as Aborigines. In New South Wales and Victoria all "part-Aborigines" were considered as Aborigines whereas from 1953 in the Northern Territory all "part-Aborigines" were explicitly excluded from being classified as Aboriginal. The assumption of Commonwealth Government powers on Aboriginal matters was much more complicated than many had anticipated and was being resisted by a number of the state governments. Despite the success of the referendum campaign, there was no rest for Kath and other FCAATSI activists, who now had a major educational program in front of them.

Their new task was to convince parliamentarians and government officials of the most appropriate way to approach the very complex question of Aboriginal advancement. She was not impressed with the publication *The Australian Aborigines* issued by the Commonwealth Department of Territories a few weeks after the referendum success. The book was extremely paternalistic and attempted to explain away the harsh and repressive policies and actions against Aborigines by the various state governments. The book was issued under the authority of the Minister for Territories and, to Kath's dismay, made the assumption that Aboriginal advancement could best be achieved through a vigorous policy of assimilation. It was obvious that the government, as well as the wider population, still had a lot to learn and Kath was more than willing to be one of the teachers. Once again Kath threw herself enthusiastically into the formidable task that lay ahead.

Although she was now spending more time on her writing which, quite often, was but another arm of her educational campaign, she was soon fulfilling dozens of speaking engagements — not only in Queensland but also in other states. Because of her growing reputation as a writer she was often in demand for interviews by reporters from the press, radio, and television. She received many requests to speak at conferences organised by service clubs, trade unions and churches. In 1974, for example, she was guest speaker at the Anglican Evangelical Conference held in Melbourne. One of the participants at the conference recalled that she laid it on the line regarding the church's neglect of, and apathy towards the Aboriginal situation. She did point out that some individual clergymen had given strong support to the Aboriginal rights movement but that the church hierarchy in general still believed that their Christian duty was to continue with welfare policies and help Aborigines assimilate into the general community. Kath pointed out that this was, in reality, a policy of cultural genocide.

Kath indicated that her most enjoyable engagements were when she could talk to schoolchildren either in small or large groups. When she visited Sydney and found that she had time to spare she would sometimes contact me to arrange a school visit for her. On one occasion she accompanied me to Sefton High School in Sydney's western suburbs. The whole school with over 1000 students was packed into the large assembly hall where Kath held the large group spellbound for some thirty-five minutes. Kath had an empathy with students that was unique. She possessed the ability to tailor her remarks to suit the needs of her audience and to make each student feel that the remarks were addressed to them alone. One of the teachers remarked that he had never seen a speaker hold the school assembly in such rapt attention for such a period of time. He added that had Kath asked if any of the students would volunteer to accompany her on a deputation to parliament to seek a better deal for the Aboriginal population, there would not have been a student left in the school.

Kath adopted her Aboriginal name of Oodgeroo, meaning paperbark tree, to confirm her growing role as a writer with international stature. She also used her appropriate Aboriginal name in her increasing role as lecturer and teacher. During the 1980s Oodgeroo was a guest lecturer at universities in both Queensland and New South Wales. Her constant theme was Aboriginal advancement through greater understanding and the need for reconciliation between the original inhabitants and the later migrants to the southern continent.

It was no surprise that Kath opened her home at Moongalba on North Stradbroke Island for educational camps for both Aboriginal and non-Aboriginal students. Some 30,000 children have participated in the educational and cultural activities involved. At Oodgeroo's funeral one of her former students, now an adult, spoke of how Oodgeroo's teachings at Moongalba had put her life back on track and gave testimony to the enormous impact Oodgeroo had on all the children who came under her care. Also, at her funeral another speaker, an Aboriginal ex-prisoner, paid special tribute to Oodgeroo's work with Aboriginal prisoners.

At the funeral, it was very clear that her work as an educator to both Aboriginal and non-Aboriginal people was of great significance to many who knew little of her international reputation as an artist and writer. Her tremendous influence as an educator will never be forgotten.

WORKS CITED

Bandler, Faith. *Turning the Tide*. Canberra: Aboriginal Studies P, 1989.
Duncan, A. T. "A Survey of the Education of the Aborigines in New South Wales." Unpubl. MEd. thesis, University of Sydney, 1969.

NOTES

1 Minutes of Federated Council for the Advancement of Aborigines and Torres Strait Islanders Annual Conference. Canberra: Federated Council for the Advancement of Aborigines and Torres Strait Islanders, 1963.
2 Background Notes for Referendum. Sydney: Aboriginal Rights "Vote Yes" Committee, NSW Branch, 1967, p. 1.

The Road Ahead

Eve Mumewa D. Fesl

Long before the British invaded Australia our people expressed their emotions, our history, the sacred and secular events of our lives, via the medium of painting, storytelling, song and ceremony.

Pre-invasion stories and songs tell of the paths of the Creation ancestors, of the history of development of our clans and nations, and the social rules which govern them. Dramas by the camp-fire re-enact the skill of the hunt, emphasise the harvesting time for foods, celebrations and teach the young technological skills. Religious ceremonies formalise in song and dance the sacred laws which dictate the daily secular behaviour for all our people — religion isn't a "one-day-a-week job".

On the fateful day that the English arrived, however, the tide of change enforced by them was to at first quell, and then almost wipe out in the South and East, the modes of expression which had survived for over 60,000 years. Monolingual English-speaking missionaries, who found it too difficult to master our languages, were the first (for purposes of evangelism), to place prohibitions on the speaking of them — penalties ranging from the washing of mouths with soap to the deprivation of food and beatings were meted out to those who elected to ignore the rule. The English missionaries also denigrated our languages (as they had done the Welsh language), as an added method of deterring our people from using the forms of communication in which they were most competent. Later, bans on the speaking of Australian languages were associated with slavery, forcing us to replace our languages with only a limited English vocabulary (Fesl 1993).

Other factors contributed to language loss, but the bans, followed by the stigmatisation of our languages, played a large part in bringing to extinction, or the brink of extinction, most of the Australian languages — a linguistic loss to the world.

For a time, our public voices were silenced, but time and fortitude, the great healers, ultimately enabled us to regain confidence and to seek other communicative means to attain justice. Oracy, which had served us well in our cultures, was transformed to oracy in English — many of our speakers were eloquent. A few outside our cultures listened, but orators can't win when seeking attention and action from those whose traditions have taught them that only the written law and the written history are valid and correct.

Under the Protection Acts which were initially legislated in 1897 and not finally repealed in their various forms until 1978, English literacy was denied to our male population and restricted to a third-grade level for the mothers and daughters of our nations who had been forced onto missions, reserves and settlements for the purposes of exploitation of their labour and seizure of their lands. Protector Roth of Queensland echoed the sentiments of those appointed under the Acts to "protect" our people:

> ... No practically useful results can accrue by our teaching our mainland blacks composition, fractions, decimals or any other subjects that will in any way enable them to come into competition with Europeans. (Fesl 107)

A consequence of the Australian Government's regulations and its actions to maintain a slave or poorly paid labour force, was that men and women in my parents' generation and those in later generations who remained incarcerated under the auspices of the Protection Acts had very little or no opportunity to develop literacy in English.

As a child, Oodgeroo and her family were among a fortunate few not part of the "settlement" system. She and her family were known as "outsiders" by the Murri community. Whether there was a stigma associated with the name "outsider", and from whose perspective is debatable. On the other hand there certainly was with the label "mission blacks" applied to those at Cherbourg (then known as Barambah) and other places where people were forced to live and provide free or menial labour for neighbouring whites.

Oodgeroo was, of course, well aware of the Protection Acts, first implemented in Queensland in 1897, legislated in all states except Tasmania by 1911 and not finally repealed in all states until 1978. "Protectors" were appointed under these Acts to force our people off their land and into the concentration camps; of them she wrote: "... There are good white men who will help us, But not the appointed and paid officials, Not the feudal police Protectors, The protectors who do not protect."

When it became painfully obvious that they needed a break from domestic work or labouring, those called "mission blacks" were sent to Dunwich for a "rest". They were boarded with the "outsiders" but had to work and look after themselves while there. Probably the "outsiders" were paid for providing this service.

Because of mixing more freely with the white community, not being a slave, having been treated comparatively well and encouraged by her school teacher, Oodgeroo developed a faith in the white community which was not shared by the "mission blacks". Her faith is reflected in one of her first poems, "The Dawn Is at Hand" which expresses hope and predicts that progress in black-white relations will occur.

Perhaps this "outsiderness" at Dunwich influenced Oodgeroo to think in international rather than parochial terms — "I'm for humanity, All one race". Despite this, it seems she faced a dilemma — on the one hand she had hope, on the other she was well aware of the injustices dealt our people. "My love is my own people first, and after that mankind". "... For there are ancient wrongs to right ... But oh, the goal is sure" (*We Are Going* 11).

In those early days her writing was to have more effect upon white people than upon black. She became a bridge between the two worlds, communicating in a language foreign to this country, the ancient beliefs and lifeways of our people. At the time of course many of our people could not read, this factor adding to the lack of influence upon us.

In 1961 the Assimilation Act had been passed. At first Oodgeroo had a belief in the rhetoric of equality which accompanied the supposed political shift. "... Make us neighbours, not fringe-dwellers. Make us mates, not poor relations ..." But slowly the reality seeped through, a sadness overwhelmed her as she believed at this time that all of our culture and all of us were to be sacrificed

for assimilation — "The corroboree is gone, And we are going
...".

Disappointment in the white community followed, "...
Namatjira, they boomed your art, They called you genius, then
broke your heart ...".

Hurt became anger. Anger at the hypocrisy of the Christian
church. Like most of our people, she was not deluded that the
message "of light" was for our benefit, but unlike others among
us at the time, she was able to articulate our feelings in writing.
A number of her poems expressed this — "... Laws of God and
laws of Mammon ... and we answered 'no more gammon'. If
you have to teach the light, Teach us how to read and write ...".
— "Holy men you came to preach; Poor black heathen, we will
teach, Sense of sin and fear of hell, Fear of God and boss as well
... We will teach you work for play, We will teach you to obey
...".

Although Oodgeroo was well received generally by the white
community, even her friend and mentor, James Devaney, insisted
that her writing be politically correct. For acceptance in the white
community she was to "entertain" only. She was to leave out
"propaganda-like stuff" and write in poetic form stories heard
from her people when she was a child. Little has changed, for while
we "entertain" we are accepted and applauded, but mention "land
rights" and the room empties but for a few. Oodgeroo tried to
comply with the request in her next book, but she slipped in "Daisy
Bindi" which dealt with slavery on Roy Hill Station.

Like a true Murri, Oodgeroo was concerned for Nature and
nature's children. "Dingo on the lone ridge, Fleeing as you spy
them, Every hand against you, May you still defy them ..." and
"... Municipal gum, it is dolorous To see you thus Set in your
black grass of bitumen — O fellow citizen, What have they done
to us?"

Oodgeroo's writing was to have a profound effect upon some
white people, for she was able to bridge the linguistic and cultural
gap that still separates the black from white citizens of this nation.

It was not until her latter years that she began to have a powerful
effect on indigenous Australians. As we became literate we realised
the power of the pen which she had demonstrated. She, along with
a handful of other writers among our people, became a role model

which I hope our young people follow. Her inspiration at Black Writers' Conferences encouraged others to take up the pen to write for justice for our people through plays, fiction, poetry and non-fiction.

Sadly, the last time we were together was at Brambuk, Gariwerd in Victoria. By now she had become a strong voice for our rights, no longer content to be politically correct for the benefit of the white population. Together we stood and addressed the conference on the Mabo legislation.

She was among the first to express our frustrations, disappointments, hope and anger at injustice in English-language literature. It was a hard and lonely road for her to tread. She had also attempted to use the white systems to benefit our people but with little success, for, while white people are dependent upon our dependency for their high wages, status positions and power, they will actively implement strategies to prevent our attaining the goal of self-management.

Now that most of us are literate in English, the young with a lifetime ahead of them must take up where Oodgeroo has left off if we are to achieve the goal of self-management which Oodgeroo finally sought.

Through the efforts of Oodgeroo, Jack Davis, and others, assistance is available to indigenous Australian writers — the Aboriginal Arts of the Australia Council offers special grants. The David Unaipon and other prizes are available to assist successful writers in having their work published.

We have had over 200 years of dominance by an English-language literate society; we now have the necessary skills so it is up to us to turn the tide. Like the road that Oodgeroo trod, the going will not be easy but with Jack Davis, Mudrooroo Narogin, Sally Morgan, Ruby Langford, Archie Weller, to name but a few of the growing number of pen-wielders amongst us who are leading the way, by the year 2000 we should have a formidable army writing for justice.

Sister, Mother and Cousin to our people,
She put in words the heartaches of us all —
Of our landscape, of the sea, of our world.
In her poetry she expressed the torments of anger —

At the treatment of our people —
The frustration of waiting for hopes
That budded, showed promise but never bloomed.

When she joined our ancestral spirits
In the arms of our Mother, the Earth
She left not a void to be filled
But a signposted path which some must follow.
The time has gone for spear and woomera to help our way
The time has come for more to use the pen
To follow along that path for Rights, that Oodgeroo has hewn.

(Eve Mumewa D. Fesl)

WORKS CITED

Fesl, Eve. *Conned*. St Lucia, Qld: U of Queensland P, 1993.
Oodgeroo Noonuccal (Kath Walker). *We Are Going*. Brisbane: Jacaranda P, 1964.
———— . *The Dawn Is at Hand*. Brisbane: Jacaranda P, 1966.
———— . *My People*. Brisbane: Jacaranda P, 1970.

Oodgeroo's Impact on Federal Politics

Robert Tickner

"...But I'll tell instead of brave and fine,
When lives of black and white entwine,
And men in brotherhood combine —
This would I tell you, son of mine"

("Son of Mine", Oodgeroo of the tribe Noonuccal)

There are few moments in contemporary Australian history that I have found more uplifting than 16 August 1991. It was on that day that, in an important moment of cross-party cooperation, the Federal Parliament gave historic unanimous support to legislation to initiate a process of reconciliation between Aboriginal and Torres Strait Islander people and the wider community. This rare political endorsement reflected the position of the reconciliation process as one of Australia's most important initiatives, lying as it does at the heart of Australia's identity as a nation. But this landmark didn't just happen. It flowed from years of determined political and public struggle by a relatively small core of Australians to bring this country closer to the achievement of social justice and equality for Aboriginal and Torres Strait Islander people. Almost a quarter of a century before the reconciliation process began, Federal Parliament provided a lead to the community when the then Coalition Government and the Labor Opposition joined to support constitutional change affecting Aboriginal people.

The people of Australia responded to the Parliament's clear message: a record 90 per cent of voters supported the 1967 referendum that gave the Commonwealth Government the power to make laws for Aboriginal and Torres Strait Islander people and for the inclusion of Aboriginal and Torres Strait Islander people in the national census. One of those who were instrumental in the campaign that led to the 1967 referendum was a small, nuggetty and outspoken woman called Oodgeroo of the tribe Noonuccal. It was Oodgeroo who, through her involvement with the Federal Council for the Advancement of Aborigines and Torres Strait Islanders (FCAATSI), was asked to go to Sydney to launch the petition for the referendum.

The passage of the 1967 referendum was the very foundation of all subsequent Commonwealth action in Aboriginal and Torres Strait Islander Affairs, including the passage of the historic Native Title legislation in December 1993. Without the resultant change to the constitution, there would have been no legal or constitutional capacity for the national Parliament to make laws directed towards Aboriginal and Torres Strait Islander people and in current times there would have been no Aboriginal and Torres Strait Islander Commission (ATSIC) and no action by the Parliament to initiate the process of reconciliation.

The fact that Oodgeroo was still in the front line 24 years later in a new era of cooperation and advancement in Aboriginal and Torres Strait Islander affairs and working to get the message of reconciliation across to the wider community is testament to her fierce determination and staying power. I first met Oodgeroo soon after I became the Minister for Aboriginal Affairs in 1990, and had the pleasure of meeting and working with her on many subsequent occasions. Reconciliation between indigenous and non-indigenous Australians was a quest that consumed Oodgeroo for much of her life. She was driven by dedication to the process, involving as it does a commitment to social justice, a program to educate the wider community about indigenous issues and consultation on a formal document of reconciliation, by whatever name, as one of the possible outcomes of the process. While the process didn't formally begin until 1991, Oodgeroo recognised reconciliation much earlier as the only true path to a united Australia. Her poetry expressed her philosophy and personal commitment to reconciliation as far back as the 1960s.

Oodgeroo's personal search for equality and social justice for her people began early in life. In the 1940s, while in her early twenties, she joined the Communist Party because it was the only party not to have the White Australia platform. In her own words:

"I joined them because I liked the way they talked...The Communists were saying that all people were born equal etc. I'd always known this, but here at long last I was hearing my party saying it." Oodgeroo soon left the Party, however, because other members wanted to write her speeches. In 1960, she became the state secretary of FCAATSI, a position which illustrated clearly the respect that Oodgeroo enjoyed from her peers.

She ran for political office in Queensland twice. The first time was in 1969, not far off her 50th birthday, as an ALP candidate for the seat of Greenslopes. The second time was in 1983 when she stood for the Democrats in the seat of Redlands. In *The Matriarchs*, Oodgeroo chronicled her lack of success in the earlier campaign. "I lost a lot of the socialist votes for two reasons. One I was a woman and two I was Aboriginal. I got a university student to do a survey on it and he said that the attitude was 'Well if we get her into Parliament we're going to be the butt of every joke that goes on around our work. To have a woman and Aboriginal at that representing us in the House.' So the Labor Party lost votes although I polled a lot of Liberal Party members because the women said we want a woman in Parliament and they backed me." Oodgeroo subsequently left the Party.

Although unable to gain office, Oodgeroo's keen interest in politics and, particularly, Aboriginal affairs remained strong throughout her life, sometimes as a thorn in the side of governments. She related in *The Matriarchs* how she was once in the office of a high-ranking bureaucrat in the then Department of Aboriginal Affairs and saw a copy of a highly controversial speech by Dr H. C. Coombs which documented the shocking levels of Aboriginal health. At the time, the conditions endured by Aboriginal people had received little publicity and the speech was marked NOT FOR PUBLICATION but, somehow, a copy of it turned up in Oodgeroo's bag. She caused much consternation when later that night, against the advice of friends, she read the speech to a gathering at Adelaide University. It is an indictment on all Australian governments that Aboriginal and Torres Strait Islander people remain, to this day, the unhealthiest Australians.

In 1985, four years prior to the establishment of the Aboriginal and Torres Strait Islander Commission (ATSIC) which today gives Aboriginal and Torres Strait Islander people the decision-making power which they had long been denied, Oodgeroo complained loudly and publicly that politicians and public servants were failing to come to grips with the Aboriginal scene. She said:

> They are making rules and regulations in their ivory towers and they know little or nothing about the grass roots situation. The failure of Australia to do justice to the Aborigines is not the fault of the Australian people. Ninety-two per cent of Australians want to give us a fair go.

In the same year, Oodgeroo was named Aborigine of the Year, an honour bestowed on her by her own people.

For all of her adult life, Oodgeroo was a keen campaigner for Aboriginal land rights and virtually all political parties have incurred her wrath on the subject at one time or another. But she knew that it was largely ignorance of Aboriginal people and their culture that was preventing her people from securing such rights. In 1986, long before the High Court's historic decision in the Mabo case, Oodgeroo captured the sentiment that this Labor Government endeavoured to communicate to the Australian people in the debate prior to the passage of the *Native Title Act 1993*. She said:

> There is a ridiculous assumption that we want Australia back. We don't want it back but, by God, we want a piece of it. We don't want one square inch of land owned by whites. We are talking about Crown land. We don't want to be rich, but we want the comfort of some security.

Oodgeroo's decision in 1988 to change her name from Kath Walker and renounce her 1970 MBE, all in protest against the Bicentennial celebrations, was not a popular one — at a time when patriotic fervour was at fever pitch. However, popularity mattered little. It was the knowledge that she had remained true to herself and to Aboriginal people that gave Oodgeroo comfort.

Throughout all of this, though, Oodgeroo *did* feel that Australia had a future worth nurturing. She knew that with knowledge came understanding. Ultimately a gentle and peaceful person, she sought to teach rather than confront. Oodgeroo's greatest hope was that today's children would lead Australia into a brighter and more harmonious future. From the time she returned to her home of Moongalba on North Stradbroke Island in the early 1970s, she taught thousands of children — Aboriginal and non-Aboriginal — about Aboriginal life and culture. ''Many European children come here all starry-eyed and wondering what it's all about,'' she said. ''They leave with a sense of fulfilment and the knowledge that there is a lot more to Australia than they have been taught at school.''

Many years ago, Oodgeroo expressed an opinion that Aboriginal and Torres Strait Islander studies should be compulsory for all students. She said that non-Aboriginal students wanted to learn about Aboriginal issues and culture but were being frustrated by a lack of teaching staff and relevant courses. It was her hope that Aboriginal and Torres Strait Islander studies would be introduced at all levels of education in her lifetime. That hope was at least partly fulfilled due to her own work. Oodgeroo was also committed to seeing that, most importantly, teachers learned as part of their regular training to teach Aboriginal and Torres Strait Islander history and culture effectively. It was at her initiative that the University of New South Wales undertook in 1992 to develop a core Aboriginal studies subject for teacher education courses, and she maintained a close involvement with the project until her death. I was pleased to give my active support to this project to teach the teachers.

Over the past few years, the subject of Aboriginal and Torres Strait Islander Studies has made its way into Australian classrooms as never before. These days, many non-Aboriginal Australian children have, during their primary and secondary education, a significant opportunity to learn about Aboriginal history and culture — certainly light-years ahead of what was taught when Oodgeroo was at school. However, she was aware that much more remains to be done and constantly urged Commonwealth, State and Territory Governments to do much more to advance the National Reconciliation and Schooling Strategy.

Through her work as an educator and her poetry, which took the Aboriginal message to millions in the wider Australian community, Oodgeroo's contribution to the process of reconciliation was virtually unparalleled. Recognition of this has come from all sides of the political spectrum.

Oodgeroo's surviving son Denis said at her funeral that if a reconciliation was achieved between Aboriginal and non-Aboriginal Australians, his mother would truly rest at peace. He said:

The main message is reconciliation and healing and peace, and the only way we are going to get that is through respect — mutual respect for our culture and all other cultures.

Oodgeroo's message lives on.

Oodgeroo's Work and Its Theatrical Potential

Sue Rider

The air was still and charged. Bodies were tense, damp. Eyes watchful. In the midst of a group of young people, an older woman was on her feet, speaking, her voice tremulous with passion:

> Old intolerance hems me round.

She took a breath and her voice gained strength.

> Insult and scorn assail.

The words were gathering momentum.

> I must be free, I must be strong
> To fight and not to fail.

A surge of energy seemed to rise from deep within her and the sound powered out.

> For there are ancient wrongs to right,
> Men's malice to endure;
> A long road —

— she pulled back to give whispered emphasis —

> — and a lonely road.

The power returned.

> But, oh, the goal is sure.
> ("My Love", *My People* 54)

As she ended, seven young voices swelled in song beside her. She stood, still, erect, face shining. And then it was over. A moment of silence, awkwardness, and all eyes settled on a small figure seated in the front row. The figure nodded, rose, muttered something and stepped forward to take the central woman in a firm embrace. Relief then. Laughter, smiles and a babble of chatter:

    "Did you really like it?"
    "Was it clear?"
    "Could you tell when —?"
    "I lost my words!"
    "I forgot to —"
    "Be all right on the night!"

It was 1984 and Kath Walker, as she was then, had just witnessed the final rehearsal of *You Came To My Country and You Didn't Turn Black*, a theatre-piece inspired by her life and work. Produced by The Acting Company of South Australia with four black and four white actors, *You Came To My Country* was a theatrical arrangement of Kath's poems linked by some of her prose with other dialogue and songs written by the company. The title came from an incident where Kath had been lecturing police cadets in Brisbane about a "wonderful multicultural day":

KATH: Now, isn't that lovely?
CADET: No! If people come to Australia, they should be prepared to be Australians.
KATH: So I told them. You came to my country and you didn't turn black.

            (*You Came to My Country*)

The result was the powerful expression of one woman's vision of her people's joy and sorrow as they strive to come to terms with alienation in a land that once was theirs.

    This was my first meeting with Oodgeroo. As director of The Acting Company, I had written to her a year before with some trepidation to broach the idea of a theatre-piece created from her work. As a non-Aborigine I had been uncertain how she would respond; would she think us patronising? impertinent? Her response was direct and unequivocal: "Marvellous. Go ahead." In the months that followed I became familiar through letter and telephone with the warmth and quick-wittedness of this spirited woman, but nothing had prepared me for the tiny powerhouse of energy and humour we met that day.

Oodgeroo had a special affinity for the stage.

Kath had flown in to Adelaide from Queensland as a guest of Adelaide Festival Writers' Week and to participate in the finishing stages of our production. She was tired and it was clearly an emotional experience for her seeing her work performed for the first time, but she soon lost no time in setting about to give advice, tips, a few pointers on meaning and expression. She spoke rapidly, emphatically, darting from one thought to another, from one actor to another. The company was rapt. Leila Rankine, herself a poet, was playing Kath. Leila had no acting experience, having only recited her own work in public before, but her performance was passionate and moving, as Kath was quick to acknowledge. Leila and the rest of the cast were intensely committed to this production, some were making personal sacrifices to take part, and to be in the presence of the woman who had given rise to the work, and whose own commitment was so vigorous and unrelenting, gave us all a deep sense of the importance and responsibility of what we were doing.

We had taken most of our source material from *My People*, grouping the poems to follow a journey from pre-invasion to white intervention through to the present. This was no conventional play. There was no plot or characterisation. The one constant point of reference was the character of Kath, sitting in her easy chair, as the other actors spoke, sang, acted and danced around her. There were loose references to Kath's life, but the structure depended on the flow of argument and linked themes rather than chronology, with much of the dramatic impact coming from the juxtaposition of particular poems or abrupt mood swings. *My People* covers a range of attitudes and points of view, from innocent joy, regret and bitterness to the inspiration of hope. Confrontation and accusation are balanced by a plea for solidarity and understanding. Once we had met Kath, such apparent contradictions made sense about a person who had been fighting for years, and still found the strength of spirit to go on. In a newspaper interview connected with the production, she said: "I can't afford the luxury of pessimism. I've got to be optimistic." This became the overriding purpose behind the whole event.

The production attracted enormous interest and went on to play to packed houses, Kath being one of our most ardent and frequent audience-members! She stayed on after the Festival to work with us on an adaptation for primary schools of her book *Stradbroke Dreamtime*, a lively recounting of her early years on North Stradbroke Island. The stories were full of humour, childhood horrors and the uncomplicated "lessons" of everyday life. Called *Kath*, the play dramatised incidents from the book, expanding with simple theatricality on the dialogue and descriptions of the original. In contrast to the plain-speaking *You Came to My Country*, this piece took an indirect approach to the issue of racism. Apart from a brief introduction explaining that two of the actors were Aboriginal, colour and race were never the focus of attention. Young audiences warmed to, laughed and gasped at Kath and the adventures of her family as they would have, given the story of any young girl. Even in discussion with the children afterwards, the actors kept to specific detail, rather than larger, abstract questions. Such an approach effectively followed the traditional story-telling method of teaching young Aboriginal children, was true to the spirit of Kath's book and, we hoped, an influential learning tool.

The play was to tour Adelaide metropolitan schools and regional South Australia as far west as Ceduna. Kath herself came on tour with us for the first two weeks. She would take great delight in giving us a mischievous wink, slipping out to lurk unseen while the play was being performed (and to have a smoke!) and then, in a moment of genuine magic, coming forward at the end from the back of the classroom, the real Kath, amid squeals and gapes from disbelieving children. Sitting not much taller than they were, she would answer questions, teach them a poem, or simply chat with them. I was struck by her unfailing liveliness and sense of timing, even within the rigours of a demanding tour schedule. She had an instinct for — and could never resist! — the theatrical moment.

Kath used to remark that she preferred to work with children because by the time people became adults "it was too late". This was the reasoning behind the Moongalba project at her home on North Stradbroke Island where she invited children from mainland Queensland to stay with her and learn about Aboriginal life and values. It was one of the gentlest and most productive ways of continuing to fight for her people in a society where racism was entrenched in the minds and laws of the people. She told me in a moment of obvious regret that she could not envisage theatre such as ours ever appearing on stage in Queensland, such was the implacability of the state political system.

Six years later, in 1990, the unthinkable had happened. There had been a change of state government and I was being asked to rework *You Came to My Country* for production under the auspices of the Queensland Museum. Not only was this a sensational turn of events, it was a marvellous opportunity to develop and improve on the first production. I was keen that this time Aboriginal input should be increased. Consulting with Oodgeroo, as she had now become, we agreed to allow the poetry to stand clear of other written links and came up with the idea of combining her poems with those of another Queensland poet, Maureen Watson, in order to broaden the focus of the original and allow for dramatic contrast of style. I would be responsible for arranging the material, again through a process of consultation, and direct the production with an all-black cast. Aboriginal co-director Kathryn Fisher was to work alongside me. Excited by the power of the poetry, Queensland Museum expanded the original concept to include an invitation to Aboriginal artists to create visual art works in response to the themes explored by Oodgeroo and Maureen Watson. The theatre-piece would be performed within the resulting exhibition in a unique celebration of Aboriginal art.

We decided to retain the intention of the original script, with the structure again encompassing a thematic journey through joy, anger, resentment and, finally, hope. This time there was no one central figure. Rather, the focus shifted with each poem, bringing different actors into prominence, taking the audience through a series of emotional vortexes in the movement from tribal to urban life. Lighting was important, and the music of Heather King, mixing traditional instruments with contemporary synthesised sound, played a significant part in the final effect of cultural timelessness.

Oodgeroo was not well, but she still made the journey from North Stradbroke to join in rehearsals and production discussion. Maureen was working in regional Queensland and could not take an active part. The stakes were higher this time. Government institutions were involved, precedents were being set. We were a company who had never worked together before. And yet, again, I found unqualified commitment from a largely inexperienced cast. Again, actors who had rarely spoken in public performed with passion and distinction. Again, the theatre-piece won critical and box-office acclaim.

It is a mark of the power of Oodgeroo's writing that it was able, in quite separate projects, to assert strength of meaning in a dramatic context and communicate that meaning to an audience, often through an untrained performer. Not every poet transfers well to the stage. Those who do give an actor clear motivation, underpinned with genuine emotion, and rhythms which accord with (though do not necessarily imitate) the patterns of speech. Maureen Watson writes to be spoken aloud. Her poetry bears the distinct influence of country and western music in its use of repetition, rhythms, rhyme schemes and colloquial language. It is essentially an oral form and its effect is immediate and emotive. The poetry of Oodgeroo is more literary, more rigorous in its exploration of craft and style; it bears detailed study and analysis, and yet each poem is clearly motivated, driven by passion that is controlled without being constrained, and maintains direct contact with the spoken voice.

It is interesting, given the innate dramatic quality of much of Oodgeroo's writing, that she was seldom drawn to write specifically for theatre. She certainly loved the theatre, had a working knowledge of it, and could herself speak poetry with an actor's flair for rhythm, timing and sense. That she was fully cognisant of the tools of drama is clear in many of her poems which gain enormous effect from such dramatic devices as dialogue, characterisation, direct address and the juxtaposition of opposing forces. She often draws on a vivid visual imagination to "set the scene", and her description of action is as clear as any stage direction. One of her major tools of communication is irony, which she connects directly to the spoken word, exploiting it with the wit and intuition of the shrewdest playwright. Indeed, in omitting to read her work aloud, it is possible to miss the humour of irony and so mistake the tone of a piece altogether. "No More Boomerang" is a case in point. Flat on the page, the message may seem hopeless and doomed:

No more boomerang
No more spear;
Now all civilised —
Colour bar and beer.

Read aloud, however, especially among a group of Aboriginal people, the increasing absurdity is a source of great amusement:

No more corroboree,
Gay dance and din,
Now we got movies,
And pay to go in.
. . . .
Abstract picture now —
What they coming at?
Cripes, in our caves
We did better than that.
. . . .
Lay down the woomera,
Lay down the waddy.
Now we got atom-bomb,
End *every*body. (32-33)

If she did not herself write drama, this has not prevented the inspiration of Oodgeroo's life and work from giving rise to several important theatre works. One of the earliest of these was *Urinchitta* (Spark of Fire), written by her younger son, Vivian Walker, some time before 1983. Vivian takes a number of Oodgeroo's poems to trace the story of Boorie, a young man, who moves from tribal beginnings into the destructive effects of white society. Boorie tries drugs and alcohol, has a stormy relationship with a white girl and argues with a group of anthropologists. Eventually, his sense of self and race pride reassert themselves, and the play ends with the "Aboriginal Charter of Rights", followed by the visionary "Song of Hope".

The play is comprised almost entirely of poems, spoken at times in their entirety by one character, sometimes split as dialogue between two or more people, sometimes simply divided between voices to give a sense of universality and range. There are detailed stage directions indicating action and setting, and a Minstrel provides music. What is fascinating for me is that, although Vivian has created a far more particularised story, his arrangement of the poems is similar to that of both versions of *You Came to My Country* and the thematic journey almost the same.

Oodgeroo's poems fall into a number of broad thematic groupings dealing with such subjects as: pre-invasion; the clash of cultures, with its concomitant violence, injustice and lack of understanding; "civilisation" and its effects; pride and "time to make a stand"; "away with bitterness" and the appeal to reason; and the move towards a "new, bright day". This sequence, in itself, contains the potential for dramatic structure. More significant for the creation of theatre is the extraordinary range of dramatic devices used by Oodgeroo in her expression of these themes.

For instance, the poems "Biami", "The Bunyip", "Nona", "Gifts", "Jarri's Love Song", "Corroboree", "Bwalla the Hunter", "Dawn Wail for the Dead", "The Young Girl Wanda" and "The Child Wife" are all concerned with life prior to white invasion. Within them, Oodgeroo's point of concentration is constantly shifting, as, like a playwright, she builds scenes, introduces characters, records dialogue, sets up opposing forces, focuses on a tiny detail. In "Biami", the simplicity of the language catches the persistent questioning of a young child and the patience of the mother's replies. It suggests a life free of complication, secure in the constancy of Biami, who is described in comfortable, familiar terms and not without humour:

> "Mother, what is that one sea,
> Sometimes blue or green or yellow?"
> "That Biami's waterhole.
> He big fellow."

We hear the energy of the child in the repeated "Mother", the rush of thought that takes two lines to express, and the profusion of words which crowd the question ("blue or green or yellow"). Contrast the mother's maturity and gentle humour as she answers in rhythms that are slower, more measured, pausing at the ends of lines, never wasting a word. Although the child takes the initiative each time, it is the mother who ends the exchange. As if conscious of the limited concentration span of her offspring, she answers one question with another and steers the child's attention in a new direction:

"Biami dug him. You see big hills all about?
They the stuff that he chuck out." (85)

A simple poem, and a gift for two actors. Follow it with "The Bunyip", which extends the situation of the adult addressing a child ("You keep quiet now, little fella") and immediately the seeds of a scene are set.

"Nona" sets another scene, one of several dealing with camp life. Here the point of view is that of someone outside the situation, watching, enjoying the course of events, someone older and more knowing than the ingenuous Nona. In stage terms this is a narrator or story-teller, making direct contact with the audience. Oodgeroo's characteristic irony is present, here untouched by bitterness, emerging in a series of apparently innocent negatives almost as unconsciously as the naked Nona moves:

And what did the men see? Ah, the men.
They did not see armlet or band
Or the bright little feather-tuft in her hair.
They had no eye for the red berries,
They did not look at these things at all. (31)

The mood is light, warm and playful, giving an actor scope for subtle humour and an exchange of looks with the audience through the unspoken suggestiveness of the final line.

Place "Gifts" after "Nona", follow it with "Jarri's Love Song", and one opens up the possibility for a sustained scene of character development and interaction. If Jarri is the young lover, and Nona the subject of his affections, then on stage this may heighten their awareness of one another during the poem "Nona". Perhaps Nona is less innocent than first appeared. Their encounter in "Gifts" takes to comic extremes the contrast between his flighty romantic fantasies and her blunt, down to earth practicality:

"I will bring you the still moonlight on the lagoon,
And steal for you the singing of all birds;
I will bring down the stars of heaven to you,
And put the bright rainbow into your hand."
"No," she said, "bring me tree-grubs." (39)

It's a marvellous deflation of the male ego. But only for a moment. "Jarri's Love Song" begins with "a sudden howl" (of joy). Now we are back to the observing story-teller and another vivid picture of camp life, with the bounding Jarri and sour old Yundi, until Jarri himself bursts in with his song. Oodgeroo's poetry has often inspired music, from the simplest melody to Malcolm Williamson's sophisticated choral arrangement of her work. "Jarri's Love Song" begs for the most artless of musical settings! Simply, it is an expression of unbridled enthusiasm, youthful clumsiness, fun, joy and, above all, love:

> But I ... got ... Nona! (62-63)

Examples of Oodgeroo's dramatic imagination abound. Still within the pre-invasion grouping there is the exquisite balance of "The Young Girl Wanda" (which we interpreted through dance), the pain of "The Child Wife", the liveliness of "Bwalla the Hunter", the atmospheric "Corroboree" and the moving "Dawn Wail for the Dead" with its evocation of early morning grief, followed by the bustle of everyday activity. She uses direct address to throw out a challenge, as in "The Past" —

> Let no-one say the past is dead

— contrasted with relaxed rhythms to suggest the deadening effects of "civilisation":

> Tonight here in suburbia as I sit
> In easy chair before electric heater. (93)

Other themes give rise to different styles: the open argument of "The Teachers" and "White Man, Dark Man", the tortured rhythms of "Racism" and "Spinners", the dignity of "We Are Going", the appeal to reason in "An Appeal", the moving liturgy of demands in "Aboriginal Charter of Rights".

The list could go on. There is often unity of period and, to some extent, purpose, yet each poem is individual in tone, point of view and specificity of content. Together, they present an array of characters, moods and actions, which transfer with vitality to the multi-dimensionality of the stage.

The most recent realisation in theatre of Oodgeroo's life and work was Queensland Theatre Company's *One Woman's Song*, written by Peta Murray and produced in 1993, the International Year of Indigenous People. Choosing to focus on Oodgeroo's broader achievements as woman, activist and writer rather than on her poetry, the play dramatises incidents from her earliest childhood to the triumphant assertion of identity that came with her taking the name Oodgeroo. The different stages of Oodgeroo's development are explored through the use of three different actors — a girl, a young woman and a mature woman — and symbolism throughout the play suggests the richness of her cultural and emotional life. The production by Queensland's State Theatre Company of *One Woman's Song* was an important celebration of the work of a woman who once regretted that her people would never receive recognition on the Queensland stage and, as it sadly happened, was a fitting tribute at the end of her life.

Oodgeroo's writing, like her life, was resonant with the passion of a woman who took on the world for her people and could still find time to give words of encouragement to the smallest child. For her there was no real distinction between performing and being; she lived life with an innate theatricality which took advantage of the moment with the instinct of an actor and the tools of a playwright. Her poems, whether ballad, elegy, dialogue, or protest song, drew on the energy and wit of the spoken word, just as her own conversation was punctuated with the images and rhythms of poetry. If all the world's a stage, then Oodgeroo was one of the major players and continues to demand a hearing.

WORKS CITED

Murray, Peta. *One Woman's Song,* 1993. Unpublished.

Noonuccal, Oodgeroo [as Kath Walker]. *My People*. 2nd ed. Milton: Jacaranda, 1981.

_____ . *Stradbroke Dreamtime*. 2nd ed. Sydney: Angus & Robertson, 1982.

_____ and The Acting Company of South Australia. *You Came to My Country and You Didn't Turn Black*. 1984. Unpublished.

_____ and The Acting Company of South Australia. *Kath*. 1984. Unpublished.

_____ , Maureen Watson, and Sue Rider. *You Came to My Country and You Didn't Turn Black*. 1990. Unpublished.

Walker, Vivian. *Urinchitta* (Spark of Fire), date unknown. Unpublished.

Performance for the People

Adam Shoemaker

Every memory has a point of departure.

My own starting point was a Wednesday in late August, 1980. The place was Minjerriba (North Stradbroke Island) off the coast of Queensland in Quandamooka (Moreton Bay), half an hour east of Brisbane. The person was the then Kath Walker, who had graciously promised to "Speak with me for a few minutes". And who was I? An eager but naive Canadian postgraduate student at the Australian National University — a stranger to Queensland; one who had only been in the country six months.

Oodgeroo took me aside in the garden of the Point Lookout Pub and gave me her undivided attention — a quarter hour in the presence of one of the most charismatic, intense and hilarious persons I had ever met. In those brief minutes, Oodgeroo mapped out the next four years of my life for me. First, she told me in no uncertain terms that I simply *had* to write a thorough study (preferably a book, but a thesis "would do" for a start) on Aboriginal writers: the "most interesting authors in all of Australia". Second, the book *had* to be based on interviews with all of the Black Australian writers I could possibly meet. Third, I was not to trust *anything* that other Australians told me about race relations, especially if they started a sentence with the words, "I'm not a racist, but . . .". As she put it, with characteristic gusto: "Most of the adults of Australia are mentally constipated . . . To hell with them! I'm writing for children from now on."

Seen in hindsight, this reflected many things. One of these was that Oodgeroo was then involved in producing *Father Sky and Mother Earth* (1981) — her first illustrated book for children. Adorned with her own colour drawings, the book gave clear voice to her environmental concerns about the dangers of the "human animal", and her hope that the younger generation would steer a path towards the future. Another aspect of this interchange was that she was beginning to trust her talent as a visual artist more openly; her ability to reach others through images as much as through words.

But the most important observation I made then was her uncanny ability to motivate and enthuse others. She undoubtedly inspired me on that day — and the same phenomenon occurred repeatedly throughout her career. Oodgeroo was a born performer, in the best sense of that word. Seen in retrospect, her whole career can be seen as a performative one in the Aboriginal tradition; one in which acting is not restricted to the theatre but is central to everyday life.

In this sense, it is not just Oodgeroo as a writer who will continue to inspire generations of Australians but Oodgeroo as an active storyteller; a central player in that high-stakes drama called Australian race relations. It is this little-remarked aspect of her life's work which I would like to concentrate upon here. I want to suggest that Oodgeroo provided a model — literally a role — for Black Australian resistance, knowledge-gathering and entertainment which travelled far beyond her writing. It was a model which was both inclusive and exclusive; tolerant and (when necessary) intolerant; peaceful and yet always activist.

This is not to say that Oodgeroo simply wore masks, that she was an actor in the western sense of the word. It is to say that her career was an extremely public one, in which image and impact were crucial. Yet, at the same time, she realised the necessity of protecting what was left of her private life and of admitting others only to appropriate levels of knowledge. The point is that Oodgeroo's political performances were masterful examples of traditional Aboriginal skills — of mime and humour — often used for strategic purposes. Throughout her career she was an extremely effective performer; one who was always a whirlwind of activities and potent ideas. And she was a true entertainer — but without any of the simplistic and pejorative connotations our society has ascribed to that word. She always entertained with cause and conviction rather than for simple amusement.

Oodgeroo was not alone in realising the importance of "the

theatre of life'' in Aboriginal society. In early 1982 Jack Davis underlined the centrality of these Black Australian skills of performance:

> You see, we've always been acting. Aboriginal people are the greatest actors in the world ... we've acted up before magistrates, we've acted up before the police, we've acted up before social workers; we've always done our own mime ... I'm sure the Aboriginal playwrights have seen that (Shoemaker 235).

In this light, acting becomes far more than physical representation; it becomes a survival skill, a technique for dealing with an often hostile or racist culture. Aboriginal dramatists such as Davis, Eva Johnson, Richard Walley and Bob Maza have shown just how potent this transference of skills can be on the stage — and, indeed, Oodgeroo's poetry has been similarly transformed in a number of stage productions.[1]

Davis is not just talking about theatrical mimesis; of merely replicating daily life on the stage. His repeated inclusion of the word ''up'' after the verb ''acted'' subtly implies that Aboriginal non-conformity is an integral part of ''performance'' before non-Aboriginal authority figures. Even more: this subversive positioning goes on all the time, everywhere in the country, as a means of negotiating the relationships between White and Black Australians. Oodgeroo was one of those who first extended this resistance into the public arena. Her political activism, her poetry, her facility with the mass media and her forays into the preserves of popular culture all deepened and strengthened the impact of this acting — and active — rebellion.

More recently, Mudrooroo has taken this pattern even further. In his recent writing he has outlined how Australian society can be conceptualised as being a script awaiting performance by actors from an indigenous ''school''; one which has been dominated up to now by a derivative British/American tradition:

> Demonstrations and tent embassies are theatrical events; political events; never worry that this white Australia eschews the political. It has reached postmodernism without passing through the modern. It has become multi-national and sold out to multi-nationals without passing through the national ... There are no more declarations of buying back the farm. Australia has become a post of infinite posts. A colonial post manufacturing ersatz nationalism from cities such

Oodgeroo at an exhibition of her original drawings, Sydney, November 1985. (Photograph by: Branco Gaica)

as Sydney. And so theatre and demonstration; tent embassy and twenty-first century; monarchy and republicanism. This Australia is a theatrical event! (Fischer 138)

According to this interpretation, the future of Australia — as a possible republic, as a potentially independent polity, as a nation which may accord equal rights to its indigenous people — is one which is in the literal process of being acted out. "Australia" becomes a potent theatrical symbol. It is like a play which is capable of being directed, performed, written into existence if Aboriginal people are given their due rights to the stage — and to the script. As such, it is the articulation of a powerful image; one which conforms to Oodgeroo's life-long dream for her people. And, committed as she was to that goal of equality and dignity, she sought the power of performance in many practical ways.

For example, in the late 1980s, as one of the artistic advisors to the Aboriginal National Theatre Trust (ANTT) Oodgeroo worked hard to cement the position of Black Australian theatre in the nation's dramatic culture. For various reasons — the onset of the recession, opposition from established theatre companies, lack of secure funding — the ANTT collapsed. However, the profile of Aboriginal theatre has undoubtedly changed and — even without an organisation like the ANTT — Black Australian drama is now firmly on the agenda of the annual Australian National Playwrights' Conference. There is no doubt that Oodgeroo, her son Kabul (formerly Vivian Walker) and other Aboriginal artists were instrumental in achieving this breakthrough.

But the stage is still just one form of theatrical presentation, as potent as it might be. Long before this, and throughout her career, Oodgeroo had been attracted to another medium — the cinema — as one which catered to her considerable skills as a visual communicator and performer. Perhaps her most striking cinematic role was her portrayal of the Aboriginal grandmother Eva in Bruce Beresford's 1986 film, *The Fringe Dwellers*. Although the production as a whole was seriously flawed, there were several memorable scenes in the film. In one particularly striking cameo, the camera focuses first upon Eva's face and then progressively upon her eyes, which are rivetting in their intensity. At the same time, the character warns her grandchildren to be careful and not to underestimate the potency of the Aboriginal spirit-world;

a parallel which highlights both the message and its delivery. As Kevin Gilbert put it, in *The Fringe Dwellers* Oodgeroo was "a powerful, spiritually moving old woman" (Gilbert 95), who re-established the honour of age with her performance.

But this was far from being Oodgeroo's first film role. One of the first Australian documentaries to deal with Aboriginal women in a non-anthropological fashion was Frank Heimans's *Shadow Sister* (1977). It became a personal, biographical showcase for Oodgeroo's words and work. She was especially delighted to win the 1977 Black Film Makers' Award in San Francisco for her performance in the film: further testimony (if any was required) of her formal acting ability. Typically, her reference to the film in interview links her personal involvement with a project for her people — and then concludes with a humorous observation:

> Frank Heimans, who has just made the film with me, *Shadow Sister*, wants to support Moongalba, if he can, through his films. Whenever I promote it he'll put me on the payroll. He also says that I'm a good actress (*laughs*) — I hope he's right, because that's where the money is. (Davidson 438)

Pride and self-deprecation mix here, as they do so often in Oodgeroo's language. And she continues to act with Jim Davidson — to play a role which effectively guides the interviewer and insists on her own agenda: the need for financial backing for Aboriginal projects; the fact that the (implicitly non-Aboriginal) cinema industry is flush with the level of funding which could support Moongalba for years.

In fact, this interview — like many others — is a classic example of Oodgeroo's performative technique. She uses the interchange as a platform and refuses to be led by questions. For example, when asked if her most famous and anthologised poem "We Are Going" implied the evanescence of Aboriginal culture she retorted:

> Yes, I thought all white men would think that: It's a double-header. Saying We Are Going was a warning to the white people: we can go out of existence, or with proper help we could also go on and live in this world in peace and harmony. It was up to the whites. Now the whites have proved to us that they're going the wrong way about it. But the Aboriginals will not go out of existence; the whites will. We are going to live; the whites are going to die. (Davidson 433)

There are obvious implications here for the interviewer. While Oodgeroo is actually saying "your interpretation is wrong" she hides the rebuttal under the generalisation "all white men", thereby giving less immediate, direct offence. However, the near-curse implied by the last line — "the whites are going to die" — is difficult to ignore; yet it is undoubtedly amusing at the same time because of its sweeping condemnation. Diplomacy and directness; humour and accusation alternate in the exchange, giving it a rhythm which is far more effective. And this is typical of Oodgeroo's highly successful skills of performance.

But there is no hiding passion when passion is required. When the interviewer touches a nerve by asking about her racial heritage, Oodgeroo's anger does flare out:

> But for God's sake! No-one recognised my white blood in me all these years — why the hell should I have to declare it now? I don't want to declare it. To hell with the white blood in me! I'm black. (Davidson 434)

To his credit Davidson printed this exchange, not shying away from conflict as many interviewers have done before him. But this does illustrate another side of Oodgeroo's dramatic repertoire: her readiness to flash into anger when anger is justified. And there is no doubt that the message is received: the interviewer's simple rejoinder "Fine, fine" speaks volumes about being surprised by the vehemence of her response. As in her poetry, Oodgeroo oscillates in this interview between empathy (for the environment, for her people) and disdain (for intolerance, or perceived ignorance). But the point is that these are not binary opposites; they emanate from the same source, the same culture, the same person, and the same Aboriginal ideology. It is certainly not as if Oodgeroo had to straddle two worlds and was uncomfortable in doing so, as the interviewer's question implies.

The cultural bifurcation model only applies if one accepts racial incompatibility as being endemic; for Oodgeroo this was simply not true. She conceptualised people (whether or not they were Black Australians) as being either pro-Aboriginal or anti-Aboriginal. And she always hoped that the latter group could be converted to a more enlightened way of seeing the world, without pandering to their prejudices along the way.

The paradox is that it is nearly impossible for one who holds strong pro-Aboriginal sympathies *not* to react to an anti-Aboriginal taunt, yet it is often that *reaction* which is characterised by other observers as being racist. Observing this trap, Oodgeroo was always clever enough to ensure the bigots were caught in their own leg-traps: she never descended to vitriol without offering an alternative. Thus, her life as a performer for her people did not involve a difficult tightrope walk between European Australia and Aboriginal Australia, as some have imagined. Rather, she played the role of one who could be the ringmaster in *anyone's* circus if she so chose; but she always did so only if she felt her Aboriginality would be respected in that environment.

Whether it was in the United States, Papua New Guinea, Nigeria, New Zealand or in China, Oodgeroo always managed to represent Aboriginal Australia first, without offending non-Aboriginal Australia in the process. Again, this was a matter of conceptualising Aboriginality as being — on different levels — both exclusive (that is, militantly proud of its own singularity) and inclusive (open and welcoming to others) at the same time.

This strategic approach to performing Aboriginality can be viewed time and time again in her career. In her speeches, Oodgeroo frequently resorted to the tactic of taking with one hand and giving with the other. For example, in a May 1968 presentation on "Integration and Queensland Society" she employed this technique with dramatic effect:

> One of Mr Wentworth's[2] pet phrases is "our Aborigines". We have to educate him to realize that we are not "his Aborigines". We are a race of people trying to uphold our dignity and pride of race, and people have got to realize this. We have our own ideas and they might be worth listening to if people took the time to get rid of the Great White Father attitude of saying "Come along, I'll do this for you"... To do this we need enlightened people from both races. (*My People* 44)

First she is accusatory, then conciliatory, then welcoming: these few lines encapsulate Oodgeroo's rhetorical technique and her oral mastery of an audience. She appeals to universal ideals of equality and self-reliance at the same time that she sketches in images of paternalism. Then the paragraph ends, significantly, with an exhortation to do something; to get involved in Aboriginal affairs. Two years later, in a speech delivered at Pius XII Seminary, in the Brisbane suburb of Banyo, Oodgeroo demonstrated another side of this performative skill: her ability to call to action all Australians on behalf of their country. Then she cleverly drove the point home by underlining the special relationship between Black Australians and that country:

> There is an urgent and immediate need to work towards a policy of salvation of the Australian land. Australia is in the grip of soulless, greedy, overseas monopolies, aided and abetted by our own politicians. For the sake of financial gain these people would rip the guts out of this beautiful country in the name of the overseas dollar. Realise this: if you kill this land you also kill the people. (*My People* 90).

There is no doubt that audiences were affected by this oratory. Repeatedly, people of all ages have commented upon Oodgeroo's eloquent ability to convince them of the rightness of her cause as being *their* cause. The key here is that she personifies the land in a way which is open to all people and then emphasises the crucial role of Aborigines as custodians of that precious resource. Thus, those two final words "the people" have a strategic double-meaning: they can refer both to "all Australians" and to "the Aboriginal people", making it nearly impossible for any listener to reject the message.

If too little attention has been given to the techniques of Oodgeroo's performative language, this is partly because of the way in which most readers have emphasised her poetry. This is understandable; however, there is little doubt that the two discourses emanate from the same creative source and are inspired by very similar ideological convictions. Hence, all of the aspects of Oodgeroo's work — her prose, her polemical speeches, her plays, her verse and her visual art — need to be seen as parts of a philosophy. That philosophy is both personal — in that it is Oodgeroo's distinctive voice — and collective — in that she always saw her role as a representative one. Above all, the philosophy was dedicated to the communication of the most lucid possible message to the widest number of people.

However, it is important not to romanticise this role. Oodgeroo never articulated a Black Australian consensus on behalf of *all* Aborigines: throughout her career she had her opponents, just as she targeted others — both black and white — for criticism. This fiction of the monolithic Aboriginal position stems from the racist illusion that all black people are alike; that Aborigines are somehow less diverse and more homogeneous in their beliefs than other human beings. It is entirely to be expected that a freedom fighter who was as vocal as Oodgeroo would be both praised and blamed; it is also entirely logical that she would have something to say herself about these verdicts.

For example, in the 1960s she was a vocal opponent of the policies of the One People for Australia League (OPAL), a conservative arm of Brisbane politics which included Aboriginal leaders such as Neville Bonner. In turn, in the early 1970s some Aboriginal spokespeople criticised her for deciding to return to Moongalba, and for giving up on an overtly activist agenda. As she put it in 1977:

> In the early stages, they felt that any Aboriginal who walked away walked out. They now realise that in order to handle the whites we have to walk away ... I was on trial, before; but now I'm really surprised when I go to places how well-liked, well-loved I am. (Davidson 436)

This sense of being judged — and also loved — by Australians continued throughout her career. For example, some opposed her decision to stand as a senate candidate in the 1983 federal election while others took her to task for withdrawing her candidacy in favour of the then Senator Bonner — and many admired her position. Her decision in late 1987 to re-claim the tribal name of Oodgeroo Noonuccal and to return her 1970 MBE as a protest against the 1988 bicentennial celebrations was seen by some as tantamount to betrayal; by others, as a brave and timely act. Then, some of those who supported her earlier protest turned against her as a hypocrite when she accepted the commission to co-write (with her son Kabul) the script for the major audio-visual presentation which was the centrepiece of the Australian Pavilion at World Expo 88 in Brisbane.

As this brief catalogue illustrates, Oodgeroo's life was as visible as it was controversial. Often she was thrust into the limelight without consciously seeking notoriety, and this necessitated a particularly resourceful strategy. She managed to navigate through these reefs by employing a skilled, theatrical response. Put another way, Oodgeroo believed that — in figurative terms — you could not change the script unless you were in the play in the first place; then you might even take over the director's chair. The symbol of the empty chair — the boycott — did not appeal to her at all. To those who criticised her for accepting "bicentennial money" by agreeing to take part in the Brisbane Expo she retorted:

> We've been picking up blood money for two hundred years — whatever comes from whites is blood money. I say pick it up and run with it and use it against them. I'm all for it. Whatever money they can get off white Australia go for it. (Turcotte 28-29)

The key words here are to "use it against them": Oodgeroo was convinced that it was a strategic advantage for Aboriginal people to conform outwardly to white Australian expectations while, at the same time, undermining the dominant culture. And she provided evidence of this flexible double-sidedness throughout her career.

On this basis, I feel it is important to discuss what is one of Oodgeroo's most unusual — and influential — pieces of writing: the Australian pavilion script which she co-wrote in 1988. Entitled *The Rainbow Serpent*, the text of the script has been in print since 1988, is readily accessible and has been purchased by readers all over the world. The eight-minute performance derived from it — a mix of music, live acting, art, and high-technology special effects — was presented some thirty times a day for the six months of the Brisbane Expo. Australian Pavilion publicity at the time estimated that over *three million* people visited the Rainbow Serpent Theatre (as it was called), during the course of the exposition.[3] Yet, the collaborative Oodgeroo/Kabul text — and its significance — have received scant critical attention up to now. Why is this so?

Some critics may have been unnerved by the perceived awkwardness or incompatibility of Oodgeroo's involvement in a world exposition during the bicentennial year, and have chosen simply to ignore the presentation as a result. Others — despite the growing strength of cultural studies in Australia — may still harbour a lingering suspicion that an eight-minute Expo pavilion performance script is slight on ideological or aesthetic grounds. Still others may not know how to handle such a text: is it theatre? Performance poetry? Oral literature? Propaganda? And there may also be a belief that a creative piece which is directly commissioned and funded by federal government departments and published by the Australian Government Publishing Service could not possibly exemplify an interesting or independent sense of Aboriginality.

I want to argue that Oodgeroo and Kabul's script for *The Rainbow Serpent* confounds these expectations. Instead of being a lame nationalistic retread of stereotypical Aboriginal images, it is a vibrant, challenging and important text. Instead of bowing to the dictates of financial backers and vested interests, the script is independent, assertive and theatrical — in the best Aboriginal sense of the word. *The Rainbow Serpent* encapsulates all of the characteristics of Oodgeroo's performative technique: her ability to censure without alienating the reader or viewer; her deep sense of pride in the uniqueness of Aboriginal identity, coupled with an invitation to learn more about that identity as a non-Aboriginal novice. In addition, the script communicates the person-to-person warmth of Black Australian relations, showcases environmental values and focuses, above all, on the Aboriginal land ethic. It is anything but marginal in the corpus of Oodgeroo's work, and demonstrates once again her flexible, creative and highly sensory approach to performance.

Without recapitulating the entire story of *The Rainbow Serpent*, it is possible to highlight salient aspects of the booklet. The text — accompanied by vivid colour photographs and artwork — is often deceptively simple; words and images blend extremely smoothly. In like fashion, the original live performance was embellished with complementary colours, lights, staging and holographic visual effects. At the outset, an Aboriginal elder greets the reader (or viewer) with the words: "Come, sit down, my country now"(2). Depending upon the way this line is read, it is capable of at least three different meanings, but all of them imply Aboriginal sovereignty. As the monologue continues, the ideology becomes clearer. Speaking of the Earth Mother, the Aboriginal actor says:

> We are different you and me . . .
> This rock and all these rocks are alive
> with her spirit. They protect us, all of us . . .
> Since the Alcheringa, that thing

you fulla call Dreamtime, this place has
given man shelter from the heat, a place
to paint, to dance the sacred dance and
to talk to his spirit.

How does one repay such gifts?

By protecting the land. (4-5)

This elegant poetry of the text is quite striking; as the Rainbow
Serpent creates the world:

She call to her Frog Tribe
to come up from their sleep
and she scratch their belly
to make them laugh. (18)

And often the rhythm is one of exhortation, or incantation:

Grow strong, Kabul, come back to your
children, the mountains, the trees and
our father the sky. Come, bring us your
birds of many colours. Come back to
your rivers rushing to Quandamooka.
Come back to your teeming fish of a
thousand colours and shapes. (22)

However, coupled with this imagery of beauty and fecundity is
a potent warning; an accusation which is directly intended for the
eyes, ears and mind of the "audience":

Kabul is the mother of us all. She is the
spirit of the land — all its beauty, all its
colour. But there are those who see no
colour, who will not feel the beauty of this
land — and who only wish to destroy the
mother and themselves. (25)

The script invokes a sense of appreciation of nature but equally
a feeling of its fragility, and especially concentrates upon the hubris
of "human animal" in a way which recalls Oodgeroo's earlier
Father Sky and Mother Earth:

And now it seems that with
all our great machines we
can travel almost
anywhere. We can travel

across the land at great
speed . . .
There is almost nothing mankind cannot do. (29-30)

But the key — the performative coup — comes on the next page.
After building up the sense of human capability (and culpability)
the authors come back with a rush to the sense of what still must
be done:

We do all these things with
the land. Good reason to
protect it. (32)

And then, the final charge is given to the reader; the responsibility
to:

Take time you earth fullas.
Let the spirit of this mighty
land touch you as it
touches my people. (34)

Is this a minor text? Clichéd? Formulaic? I would argue exactly
the opposite: especially when combined with its live performance
The Rainbow Serpent was, and is, an important example of
specifically Black Australian theatre and the ideology of
independent Aboriginality. In 1988, all visitors to the Australian
Pavilion not only heard and saw the text but were also welcomed
by the recorded voice of Oodgeroo, while their eyes adjusted to
the dimmed light of the pavilion theatre. In other words, they
received Oodgeroo on all frequencies and through all their senses.
In its totality, the co-production is an excellent example of her
skills, her innovation and, above all, her performative strategy.

I feel that at base, and throughout her career, Oodgeroo was
a consummate performer. This has been little understood and even
less appreciated. But there is little doubt that all of her
achievements involved a delicate, strategic and often ingenious
deployment of performative skills — and those derived directly
from her Aboriginal heritage, her sense of land and place. As
Bruce McGuinness described the process, in 1983:

When Aboriginal people write they write in a style. They're able to
adopt various styles of writing so that what they really want to write
about is there. It's hidden. It's contained within their writing, if one

can go through the subterfuge, camouflage that they use when they're writing ... they become actors in fact. (Davis and Hodge 47)

It is difficult to find a more lucid description of Oodgeroo's writing and acting strategy. She was, over and over, an actor — in fact, and with tremendous effect. The final proof is that long after her death, the roles she established for Black Australians, the sense of the possible which she gave to all who knew her, will be played and replayed for generations.

WORKS CITED

Davidson, Jim. "Interview: Kath Walker." *Meanjin* 36.4 (1977): 428-41.

Davis, Jack, and Bob Hodge, eds. *Aboriginal Writing Today*. Canberra: AIAS, 1985.

Fischer, Gerhard, ed. *The Mudrooroo-Müller Project: A Theatrical Casebook*. Sydney: NSWUP, 1993.

Gilbert, Kevin, ed. *Inside Black Australia*. Ringwood: Penguin, 1988.

Noonuccal, Oodgeroo (as Kath Walker). *Father Sky and Mother Earth*. Brisbane: Jacaranda, 1981.

———. *My People: A Kath Walker Collection*. Brisbane: Jacaranda, 1970.

———., and Kabul Oodgeroo Noonuccal. *The Rainbow Serpent*. Canberra: AGPS, 1988.

Shoemaker, Adam. "An Interview with Jack Davis." *Westerly* 4 (1982): 111-16.

Turcotte, Gerry. "Recording the Cries of the People: An Interview with Oodgeroo (Kath Walker)." *Aboriginal Culture Today*. Ed. Anna Rutherford. Sydney: Dangaroo, 1988: 16-30.

NOTES

1   For a fuller treatment of this topic, see the essay by Sue Rider in this collection.
2   W. C. Wentworth was at that time the federal Minister for Aboriginal Affairs.
3   This figure was provided in the October 1988 issue of *Expo Update*, a regular circular of information produced by the World Expo 88 Authority.

Oodgeroo: A Selective Checklist

Janine Little

Oodgeroo Noonuccal described herself as an educator and
storyteller, as well as a poet. Her poetic legacy is prolific and well
documented, but as a committed voice of her people Oodgeroo
utilised many other media. This checklist illustrates Oodgeroo's
versatility across written, spoken and visual media, and provides
a guide to critical and artistic perspectives of her life and work.
It is important to emphasise the oral nature of this work, as
Oodgeroo herself did, and the checklist has included items that
may offer some insight into the strong oral base of her poetry,
speeches and stories. It is unfortunate that Oodgeroo's hundreds
of speeches at conferences, classes at Moongalba, educational
institutions and other public occasions, remain undocumented.
Oodgeroo often spoke without any written material, and thus the
only record of these speeches may be the memories of those who
heard her speak.

Sections A and B of the checklist detail chronologically
Oodgeroo's published collected verse, prose and other writings.
Reviews of Oodgeroo's collected verse are restricted to journals
and, in the case of newspapers, to the weekend issues of the
Australian, *Age* and *Sydney Morning Herald*, as per the *ALS*
Annual Bibliography (obituaries are an exception). In Section B,
it was not possible in every case to determine the form of the work,
but Oodgeroo herself did not always categorise her writing by
genre. Indeed, much of it resists classification and this section does
not attempt to do so. It does attempt to indicate where her work
is published and the anthologies to which she contributed. Section
C lists critical works about Oodgeroo, arranged alphabetically and
including publications in journals, some popular magazines, press

as for Section A, and some conference papers. It focusses on Australian sources, but includes international listings where available. Only books that have a substantial mention of Oodgeroo are included in this section.

Section D will be of particular value to studies of Oodgeroo that aim to enhance her reputation as a gifted orator, performer and artist. It is an alphabetical list of sound recordings, film, radio and television programs featuring Oodgeroo, and performances about her. Unless otherwise indicated, items are held in the Audiovisual Library at the University of Queensland. Again, these items offer some indication of Oodgeroo's strong oratorical abilities, as well as her commitment as an activist in Aboriginal affairs, and an ambassador for her country. The international acclaim she receives for this commitment, and her literary standing, means that the obituary list (Section E) is inevitably incomplete.

The checklist was compiled through the resources of The University of Queensland's Fryer, Central and Audio-Visual libraries. Austlit and APAIS databases were cross-checked with the *Australian Literary Studies* Annual Bibliographies. The checklist does not list individual verse by Oodgeroo, since a search on Austlit, verse inclusive, yielded more than 10,300 entries. In contrast, a search on the MLA database was disappointing in that it provided only three items by or about Oodgeroo (or Kath Walker, Oodgeroo Noonuccal, or Oodgeroo Nunukul). The AARNET database was used to search catalogues at the Australian National Library and Griffith University library (which holds a minor collection of work by Oodgeroo). The Fryer Memorial Library holds an extensive archive of Oodgeroo's manuscripts and personal papers, along with approximately ten hours of taped interviews with her. Personal correspondence from, to and about Oodgeroo are held in other manuscript archives and private collections. The Frank Hardy Papers (Australian National Library, Canberra) and the Ray Verrills Collection (Editor, *The Realist Writer*, personal papers) are two significant sources. A sizeable collection of manuscript material remained at Moongalba (Oodgeroo's home) after her death. It is hoped that these papers will be deposited in the Fryer archive.[1]

The following abbreviations are used:

ABR   *Australian Book Review*
ALS   *Australian Literary Studies*
A&R   Angus and Robertson
NLR   *New Literatures Review*
SPACLALS South Pacific Association for Commonwealth
          Literature and Language Studies
SMH   *Sydney Morning Herald*
TLS   *Times Literary Supplement*
UQP   University of Queensland Press
WLWE   *World Literatures Written In English*

SECTION HEADINGS

A: Collected Verse and Prose by, and Reviews about, Oodgeroo
B: Prose, Writings and Other Works by Oodgeroo
C: Critical Works about Oodgeroo
D: Audio-Visual and Performance Material Featuring Oodgeroo
E: Obituaries

A: Collected Verse and Prose by, and Reviews about, Oodgeroo

We Are Going: Poems. Brisbane: Jacaranda P, 1964.
Reviewed by A. Brissenden, "Forty Years On." *Southerly* 24 (1964): 248-49;
TLS 10 Sep. 1964: 842; Jill Hellyer, *Hemisphere* 7.12 (1964): 17-18; Dorothy
Jones, *Poetry Magazine* 3 (1964): 31; Ian Turner, *Australian* 26 Sep. 1964;
Ronald McCuaig, *Bulletin* 22 August 1964: 52; D. Douglas, *Age Literary
Review* 8 August 1964: 22; *Literary Letter* April (1964): 5.

The Dawn Is at Hand. Brisbane: Jacaranda P, 1966.
Winner of The Jessie Lichfield Award for Literature 1967.
Reviewed by Leon Cantrell, *Poetry Magazine* 1 (1967): 31-32; B. Gill,
Australian 5 Nov. 1966: 9; S. E. Lee, *Southerly* 27 (1967): 60-71; Roland
Robinson, *SMH* 12 Nov. 1966: 20; Thomas Shapcott, *ABR* 6 (1966-67): 33;
Andrew Taylor, *Overland* 36 (1967): 44; Ronald McCuaig, *Literary Letter*
42 (1966): 4.

My People: a Kath Walker Collection. Brisbane: Jacaranda P, 1970. Includes
all poems in previous two collections plus nine new poems. Rpt. 1981.
Reviewed by S. E. Lee, *Southerly* 31 (1971): 233-34; R. Hall, *Australian* 24 April
1971: 20; Roland Robinson, "Poetry of Anger." *Makar* 7.1 (1971): 7-9; Nick
Wilkinson, *New Guinea* 6.3 (1971): 62; *Union Recorder* 51.3 (1971): 7.

Stradbroke Dreamtime. Pymble, NSW: A&R, 1972. Republished with
annotations by Atsuko Onogi and Michio Ochi (Yokohama: Mondo Books,
1972). 2nd ed. with illustrations by Lorraine Hannay, 1982.
Reviewed by M. Dunkle, *ABR* 31 (1981): 34-36; S. Lees, *The Review*
(Melbourne) 24-30 June 1972: 1025; D. Moore, *Bulletin* 3 June 1972: 52;
R. Robinson, *SMH* 3 June 1972: 21; *TLS* 14 June 1972: 13; Walter McVitty,
Age 16-17 Oct. 1982: 12, David Moore, *Bulletin* 3 June 1972: 52; *Southern
Cross* 3 (1982): 15.

Father Sky and Mother Earth. Written & illustrated by Oodgeroo. Brisbane: Jacaranda P, 1981.

Little Fella: poems by Kath Walker. Illustrated by Shirley Downing. Darwin, NT: Pee Wee Series 11, NT Dept. of Education, 1987.

Kath Walker in China. Trans. Gu Zixin. Foreword by Manning Clark. Brisbane: Jacaranda P and International Culture Publishing Corp., 1988. Reviewed by S. Patton, *ABR* 122 (1990): 13; Glen Jennings, *Arena* 95 (1991): 170-73; Elizabeth Smith, *Queensland Writer* 2.1 (1990): 17.

The Rainbow Serpent: Oodgeroo Noonuccal and Kabul Oodgeroo Noonuccal. Canberra: AGPS, 1988. Presented at the Australian Pavillion, World Expo 88, Brisbane.

My People: Oodgeroo. Brisbane: Jacaranda P, 1990.

Nunukul [sic]. *Stradbroke Dreamtime*. Pymble, NSW: A&R, 1992. Reviewed by "Black View." *Weekend Australian* 29-30 Aug. 1992: Review 6; Margaret Dunkle, "Forecasts." *Australian Bookseller and Publisher* 73.1040 (1993): 42.

Oodgeroo Noonuccal, ed. *Australian Legends and Landscapes*. Illustrated by Reg Morrison. Milson's Point, NSW: Random Century, 1990.

Stradbroke Dreamtime. Illustrated by Bronwyn Bancroft. Rev. ed. Pymble, NSW: A&R, 1993.

B: Prose Writings and Other Works by Oodgeroo

"Political Rights for Aboriginals." *Aboriginal Quarterly* June (1969): 9.

"A Plea for Tolerance." Rev. of *The First Born and Other Poems*. By Jack Davis. *Makar* 7.1 (1971): 41-42.

"Koo-Poo." *Identity* 1.4 (1972): 30.

"Moongalba." *Identity* 1.4 (1972): 11-12.

"Some Black and White Racist Attitudes." Rev. of *Because a White Man'll Never Do It*. By Kevin Gilbert. *Nation Review* March 29-April 4 1974: 760.

"Tail of a Platypus." *Identity* 1.10 (1974): 34.

"The Rosary Beads." *Identity* 2.2 (1974): 29.

"Aboriginal Literature." *Identity* 2.3 (1975): 39-40.

"Flight into Tunis." *Identity* 2.4 (1975): 6-8.

"Interview." *Meanjin* 36.4 (1977): 428-41.

"A Look at the Seventies." Report of a speech. *Identity* 3.11 (1979): 6.

Yalbilinga (to learn). Sydney: ABSCOL UNSW, 197-?

"Today's Plays." *Hemisphere* 26.2 (1981): 107.

"Aboriginal Betrayal: Land Rights (Makarata)." (Poster). Brisbane: n.p, 1981.

"We Look After Our Own." [in Chinese]. *Oceanic Literature* 4 (1982): 116-21.

"Opening Address." The Second Aboriginal Writers' Conference. Melbourne, Nov. 1983. Published in *Hecate* 9 (1983): 141; *Writing From The Fringe: A Study of Modern Aboriginal Literature*. By Mudrooroo Narogin. Melbourne: Hyland House, 1990. 21-23.

"Hijack."; "I Used My Art For Sanity's Sake." *Long Water: Aboriginal Art and Literature*. Eds. Ulli Beier and Rudi Krausmann. A special edition of *Aspect* 34 (1986): 83-86, 52-57.

"Why I am now Oodgeroo Noonuccal." *Age* 30 Dec 1987: 2.

"My Day." *Woman's Day* 17 July 1988: 85.

"Paperbark Tree." *Aboriginal Culture Today*. Ed. Anna Rutherford. Sydney: Dangaroo P, 1988. 31-32.

"The Turtle." *Eclipsed: Two Centuries of Australian Women's Fiction*. Eds. Connie Burns and Marygai McNamara. Sydney: Collins, 1988. 334-48.

"What is there to Celebrate." *Australian Writing Now*. Eds. Manfred Jurgensen and Robert Adamson. Ringwood, Vic.: Outrider/Penguin, 1988. 33-35.

Towards a Global Village in the Southern Hemisphere. Nathan, Qld: Institute for Cultural Policy Studies, Division of Humanities, Griffith University, 1989.

Oodgeroo Noonuccal, Reg Morrison and Paul Cliff. *The Spirit of Australia: the Finest Photographs of Reg Morrison*. Text by Oodgeroo and Paul Cliff. Silverwater, NSW: Golden P, 1989.

"Custodians of the Land." (Speech given by Oodgeroo when presented with an Honorary Doctorate from Humanities Faculty, Griffith University, Brisbane, 22 Apr. 1989.) *My People*. 1990 ed. 103-09.

"Interlude." *My People*. 1990 ed. 63-64.

"Note." *Paperbark: A Collection of Black Australian Writings*. Eds. Jack Davis, Mudrooroo Narogin, Stephen Muecke and Adam Shoemaker. St Lucia, Qld: UQP, 1990. vii-ix.

"Oodgeroo Noonuccal: Writer, Poet and Educator." *Aboriginal Voices: Contemporary Aboriginal Artists, Writers and Performers*. Ed. Liz Thompson. Brookvale, NSW: Simon & Schuster, 1990. 154-58.

"Summer." *My People* (1990). 89-93.

"Legend of Mooloomba (Point Lookout)." *Australian Legends*. Oodgeroo. 23-25.

"Legends of the Noonuccal and Nooghie Tribes." *Australian Legends*. Oodgeroo. 29-30.

"Merripool — Caller of the Winds." *Australian Legends*. Oodgeroo. 17-18.

Australia's Unwritten History: More Legends of Our Land. Sydney: Harcourt, Brace, Jovanovich, c1992.

"Mumma's Pet." *Goodbye To Romance: Stories by Australian and New Zealand Women Writers*. Eds. Elizabeth Webby and Lydia Wevers. Sydney: Allen & Unwin, 1989. 181-84. Rpt. in *Stradbroke Dreamtime* (1992). 42-46.

"The Tank." *Identity* 1.1 (1971): 35-36. Rpt. in *Stradbroke Dreamtime* (1992). 14-18.

C: Critical Works About Oodgeroo

"Aboriginal Kath Walker Accuses." *Identity* 3.4 (1977): 9.

"Aboriginal Poet's First Edition Sold Out." *Literary Letter* May (1964): 2.

Anderson, Michael. "A Call for Justice." *Identity* 1 (1973): 8.

"An Interview With Kath Walker." *Aspect* 5 (1963): 7-11.

Arens, Werner. "The Image of Australia in Australian Poetry." *Australian Papers*. Ed. Mirko Jurak. Ljubljana (Yugoslavia): Faculty of Arts and Science, Edvard Kardelj University of Ljubljana, 1983. 217-36.

Baker, Candida. "Kath Walker." *Yacker 2: Australian Writers Talk About Their Work*. By Candida Baker. Woollahra, NSW: Pan, 1987. 280-301.

Beaver, Bruce. "Australian Letter." *Landfall* 19 (1965): 368-72.

Beier, Ulli. *Quandamooka: The Art of Kath Walker*. Bathurst, NSW: Robert Brown/Aboriginal Artists Agency, 1985.

Beston, John B. "The Aboriginal Poets in English." *Meanjin* 36.3 (1977): 446-61.

Bourke, Lawrence. "Maori and Aboriginal Literature in Australian and New Zealand Poetry Anthologies: Some Problems and Perspectives." *NLR* 25 (1993): 23-28.

Boyd, Roger. "Aboriginal Literature." *Words'Worth* 20.1 (1987): 20-26.

Brownsey, Lynda. "The Eikon of the Holy Spirit Our Mother Spirit: Dilly Bag Theology." *Women-Church* 13 (1993): 44-48.

Clark, Ross. "Written with Blood and Black Ink." *Scope* 26.6 (1982): 1-2.

Cockington, James. "True Confessions: Who Cares about the Environment?" *Good Weekend* 11-12 February 1989: 9-10.

Dale, Leigh. "Lights and Shadows: Poetry by Aboriginal Women." *Poetry and Gender: Statements and Essays in Australian Women's Poetry and Poetics.* Eds. David Brooks and Brenda Walker. St Lucia, Qld: UQP, 1989. 73-82.

Davis, Jack. "Aboriginal Writers." [Condensed from paper given at 42nd PEN Conference, Sydney, 1977.] *Identity* 3.8 (1978): 16-17.

Davidson, Jim. "Interview — Kath Walker." *Meanjin* 36.4 (1977): 428-41. Rpt. *Sideways from the Page: The Meanjin Interviews.* Sydney: Fontana-Collins, 1983. 52-70.

Dexter, Nancy Nugent. "Kath's in Town with a Few Bitter Truths." *Age* 30 July 1975: 19.

Diesendorf, Margaret. "Black Poets of Australia." *Creative Moment* 2.1 (1973): 7-17.

Doobov, Ruth. "The New Dreamtime: Kath Walker in Australian Literature." *ALS* 6.1(1973): 46-55.

Faulkner, Heather. "Rainbow Spirit." *Australian Way* July (1988): 26-30.

Ferrier, Carole. "'Written Out of This Text'? The Reception of Some Aboriginal Women's Writing." Paper presented at the *Voices of a Margin: Speaking For Yourself* Conference, University of Central Queensland, Rockhampton (Qld), Dec. 1993.

Fox, Len. "Kath Walker: Aboriginal Poet." *Realist Writer* 16 (1964): 24-25.

Gilbert, Pam. "Antigone Kefala and Marginalisation in Australian Literature: Postscript." *Coming Out from Under: Contemporary Australian Women Writers.* By Pam Gilbert. Sydney: Pandora, 1988. 187-200.

Gostand, Reba. "Oodgeroo Noonuccal." *Social Alternatives* 12.4 (1994): 9.

Grassby, Albert Jaime. *Oodgeroo Noonuccal: Poet, Painter and Elder of Her People.* Illustrated by Bruce Smith. South Melbourne: Macmillan, 1991.

Guthrie, Richard. "Two Weeks of Hope." *Cinema Papers* 62 (1987): 43.

Harford, Sonia. "Positive Protestor." *Australian Way* July (1993): 89-91.

Harris, Michael. "The Aboriginal Voice in Australian Poetry." *Antipodes* 4.1 (1990): 4-8.

Healy, J. J. "The True Life in Our History: Aboriginal Literature in Australia." *Antipodes* 2.2 (1988): 79-85.

―――― . "Ethnogenesis, the state and the beginnings of Aboriginal literature in Australia." *Australian and New Zealand Studies in Canada* 8 (1992): 1-17.

Healey, Ken. "Black Playwrights' Conference." *Centre Stage* 1.6 (1987): 7-8.

Higham, Charles. "The Fictionaires." *Bulletin* 25 Feb. 1967: 17-20.

Hogan, Christine. "Kath Walker — An Extraordinary Life." *Portfolio* July (1987): 14-15.

Indyk, Ivor. "Assimilation or Appropriation: Uses of European Literary Forms in Black Australian Writing." *ALS* 15.4 (1992): 249-60.

_____ . "Pastoral and Priority: The Aboriginal in Australian Pastoral."
    New Literary History 24.4 (1993): 837-55.
Jennings, Glen. "Travels in China." *Arena* 95 (1991): 170-73.
"Kath Walker Retires." *Australian* 8 June 1971: 7.
Knudsen, Eva Rask. "Fringe Finds Focus: Developments and Strategies in
    Aboriginal Writing in English." *European Perspectives: Contemporary
    Essays on Australian Literature*. [*ALS* 15.2] Eds. Giovanna Capone,
    Bruce Clunies-Ross & Werner Senn. St Lucia, Qld: UQP, 1991. 32-44.
Langford, Ruby (Ginibi). "Koori Dubays." *Heroines: A Contemporary
    Anthology of Australian Women Writers*. Ed. Dale Spender. Ringwood,
    Vic.: Penguin, 1991. 131-41.
Lauer, Margaret Read. "Kath Walker at Moongalba: Making the New
    Dreamtime." *WLWE* 17.1 (1978): 83-95.
"Leading Poet Visits Oatley Campus." *Uniken* 294 (14 Sep. 1990): 8.
Lynch, Paul. "Poet's Tribe Challenges Cook's Act of Possession." *Australian*
    7-8 May 1988: 3.
Mason, Bobbie Ann. "Kath Walker: Aboriginal Poet." *Denver Quarterly*
    15.4 (1981): 63-75.
Maurer, Tracey. "A Poet's Debt to 'Godless' Ancestors." *Australian* 16 Oct.
    1987: 3.
McCredie, Jane. "Black Poet Thankful for Life between Two Worlds." *Age*
    3 Oct. 1981: 16.
McKenna, Hazel. "Aboriginal Studies Hand Oodgeroo Last Laugh." *Weekend
    Australian* 16-17 Jan. 1993: 1-2.
Miller, Rodney G. "Rhetoric of Resentment: Protest in Two Contemporary
    Aboriginal Writers." Paper delivered on 19 May 1977 at SPACLALS
    Conference, U of Qld.
Mudrooroo (Colin Johnson). "A Literature of Aboriginality." *Ulitarra* 1
    (1992): 28-33.
_____ . "White Forms, Aboriginal Content." *Aboriginal Writing Today*.
    Eds. Jack Davis and Bob Hodge. Canberra: Aust. Institute of Aboriginal
    Studies, 1985. 21-33.
Narogin, Mudrooroo. *Writing From The Fringe: A Study of Modern
    Aboriginal Literature*. Melbourne: Hyland House, 1990.
_____ . "Paperbark." *Aboriginal Culture Today*. Ed. Anna Rutherford.
    Sydney: Dangaroo P, 1988. 36-49.
Neller, Shelley. "Kath Walker, Activist, Artist Finds a New Medium for Her
    Cause." *Bulletin* 3 Dec. 1985: 88-90.
Nelson, Emmanuel S. "Black America and the Australian Aboriginal Literary
    Consciousness." *Westerly* 30.4 (1985): 43-54.
_____ . "Struggle for a Black Aesthetic: Critical Theory in Contemporary
    Aboriginal Australia." *Australian Studies* (UK) 6 (1992): 29-37.
Neumann, Klaus. "A Postcolonial Writing of Aboriginal History." *Meanjin*
    51.2 (1992): 277-98.
"Notes and Change." *Scope* 28.3 (1984): 3.
Nugent, Ann. "Spirit of Place: The First National Black Playwrights'
    Conference." *Age Monthly Review* 6.11 (1987): 10-11.
Peake, Ross. "Democrats Click [sic] to the Main Chance" *Australian*
    21-22 May 1982: 9.
"Recent Events." *Notes and Furphies* 12 (1984): 15.
Riemenschneider, Dieter. "Australian Aboriginal Writing in English: The
    Short Story." *Antipodes* 4.1 (1990): 39-45.

Roberts, Greg. "Kath Walker Makes a Stand in the Sitting Down Place." *Good Weekend* 28 Feb. 1987: 18-21, 23.

Rubbo, Mark. "Starters and Writers." *ABR* 72 (1985): 2.

Scott, L.E. "The Lady in Black Seeking Truth in the Night." *Pacific Quarterly Moana* 4.4 (1979).

"Shadow Sister." *Womanspeak* 3.3 (1977): 16-17.

Shapcott, Thomas. "The Good Word and the Hard Word." *Arts Queensland* 1.4 (1984): 28.

Sheridan, Susan. "Women Writers." *The Penguin New Literary History of Australia.* Ed. Laurie Hergenhan. Melbourne: Penguin, 1988. 319-36. *ALS* 13.4 (1988).

Shoemaker, Adam. "Aboriginal Literature." *The Penguin New Literary History of Australia.* Ed. Laurie Hergenhan. Melbourne: Penguin, 1988. 27-46. *ALS* 13.4 (1988).

_____ . "The Poetry of Politics: Australian Aboriginal Verse." *Black Words, White Page: Aboriginal Literature 1929-1988.* By Adam Shoemaker. St Lucia, Qld: UQP, 1989. 179-229.

_____ . "Aboriginal Patriots: Kevin Gilbert and Oodgeroo Nunukul [sic]." *Notes and Furphies* 31 (1993): 1-2.

Smith, Elizabeth. "Are You Going to Come Back Tomorrow?" *The Queensland Writer* 2.1 (1990): 13-16.

Solomon, Robert. "Two Peoples Join Hands in a Marriage of the Arts." *Australian* 21 Apr. 1992: 10.

Stilz, Gerhard. "Topographies of the Self: Coming to Terms with the Australian Landscape in Contemporary Australian Poetry." *European Perspectives: Contemporary Essays on Australian Literature. [ALS* 15.2] Eds. Giovanna Capone and Werner Senn. St Lucia, Qld: UQP, 1991. 55-71.

Syson, Ian. "Working Class Literature Without Class?" *Social Alternatives* 12.3 (1993): 25-29.

Sweetman, Kim. "The Australian Book Fair 1993." *Incite* 14.3 (1993): 7.

"The Australian Book Fair 1993: to be opened by Oodgeroo Noonuccal, A Great Australian." *In Sight* 14.3 (April 1993): 7.

Taylor, Andrew. "Writers Week, Adelaide Festival." *ABR* 78 (1986): 19-20.

Tiffin, Chris. "Look to the New Found Dreaming: Identity and Technique in Australian Aboriginal Writing." *Journal of Commonwealth Literature* 20.1 (1985): 156-70.

Trenoweth, Samantha. "Dreaming a New World: Interview with Oodgeroo Noonuccal." *Simply Living* 6.5 (1992): 15-18.

Turcotte, Gerry. "Recording the Cries of the People." *Aboriginal Culture Today.* Ed. Anna Rutherford. Sydney: Dangaroo P, 1988. 16-30.

Urban, Andrew L. "Kath Walker is Finding Solace in Sea Creatures." *Australian* 21 Nov. 1986: 16.

Van Oudtshoorn, Nic. "Poet and Painter: Poet Kath Walker Takes Aboriginal Art Back to Its Roots." *People* July (1981): 48-49.

Visontay, Michael. "Five Angry Women with Many Wrongs to Write." *SMH* 3 Sep. 1988: 83.

Wallis, John. "Kath Walker: Poetry or Propaganda?" *Checkpoint* 10 (1972): 22-24.

Watego, Cliff. "Aboriginal Poetry and White Criticism." *Aboriginal Writing Today.* Canberra: Aust. Institute of Aboriginal Studies, 1985. 75-90.

_____ . "Backgrounds to Aboriginal Literature." *Connections: Essays on Black Literatures*. Ed. Emmanuel S. Nelson. Canberra: Aboriginal Studies P, 1988. 11-23.

Weiniger, Peter. "Kath Walker and the New Dreamtime." *Age* 18 Aug. 1980: 11.

Westwood, Matthew. "Oodgeroo Burial a 'Celebration of Life'." *Australian* 21 Sep. 1993: 3.

Wright, Judith. "The Koori Voice: A New Literature." *Australian Author* 5.4 (1973): 38-44.

_____ . "Two Dreamtimes (for Kath Walker)." *Alive: Poems 1971-72*. By Judith Wright. Cremorne, NSW: A&R, 1973. 22-24. Also in *A Human Pattern: Selected Poems*. By Judith Wright. North Ryde, NSW: A&R, 1990. 166-69; *My People: Oodgeroo*. By Oodgeroo Noonuccal. Brisbane: Jacaranda P, 1990. 109-12.

Yahp, Beth. "A Night Oodgeroo Would Have Relished." *SMH* 18 Sep. 1993: 11.

D: Audiovisual and Performance Material Featuring Oodgeroo

Unless otherwise indicated, items are held in the Audiovisual Library at the University of Qld.

Conversation with Kath Walker. Audiotape. Hazel de Berg Collection, Australian National Library. Oodgeroo talks about *The Dawn Is at Hand* and *We Are Going*, reads "Son of Mine", "Biami" and "The Past". 10 March, 1976. 1 tape, 45 mins, transcript.

Dream Time — Machine Time. Writ. Joanna Penglase. Prod. and Dir. Don Featherstone. Presented by Justine Saunders and Brian Syron. Sydney: ABC, 1989. 60 mins.

Festival Poets. With Peter Goldsworthy. Poet's Tongue Series. Sydney: ABC, 1984. Rec. 10 June 1984. Writers' Week, Adelaide Festival of Arts. 20 mins.

The Greening Years. Interviews with Oodgeroo, Harry Butler, Robyn Archer, Donald Horne, Betty Archdale and Don Dunstan. Sydney: ABC, 1982. 3 audiotapes. 180 mins.

Is there anything to celebrate in 1988? Prod. Pat Kavanagh. Forum chaired by Michael Mansell with Oodgeroo, Gary Foley, Naomi Mayers, Rob Riley, Jo Willmot, Bob Weatherall and Pat Dodson. Sydney: ABC, 1985. 60 mins.

"Kath Walker: A Tribute." Audiotape. Mt Larcom (Qld): Mt Larcom State High School, 197-? 4 mins.

"Kath Walker." *This Is Your Life*. Series 6. Episode 1. Sydney: Lifetime Association, 1980. 30 mins.

"Kath Walker." (Kit: 24 slides, 1 audiotape, 1 booklet). *Famous Australian Women Series*. Prahran, Vic.: Equality P, 1987.

Mudrooroo. Untitled. Performance poem in memory of Oodgeroo, "Minjerriba Tribute: Celebrating Australia's Black Writers." Minjerriba (Stradbroke Island), 30 Sep. 1993.

Murray, Peta. "One Woman's Song." Dir. Janet Robertson. Dramatic performance biography of Oodgeroo. Brisbane: Qld Theatre Co., 27 May-26 June 1993.

Oodgeroo, actor. *The Fringe Dwellers*. Film adaptation of Nene Gare novel. Dir. Bruce Beresford. Jolimont, Vic: Fringe Dwellers Productions, 1986. 98 mins.

Oodgeroo, Henry Lawson, Henry Kendall; Royston Nicholas (singer). *Australian Poetry: a musical recitation*. n.p: 197-? 45 mins.

Oodgeroo. "A Story of Hope." Audiotape. Reading four variations of the poem set to music. 6 mins.

"Oodgeroo Noonuccal — A Life." *Life Series*. With Peter Ross. Sydney: ABC, 16 Dec. 1992. 25 mins.

Schwenke, Julianne. Kath Walker interviewed. Audiotapes. Brisbane: n.p, 197-? 7 audiotapes. 630 mins.

Shadow Sister. Sydney: Cinetel Productions. Prod. Dir. Ed. Frank Heimans. Written by Oodgeroo and Frank Heimans. Biographical film, Nth Stradbroke Island. 1977. 16mm, 52 mins.

Tripcony, Paul. Kath Walker talks to Paul Tripcony. Audiotape. Stradbroke Island: n. p, 1973. 60 mins.

E: Obituaries

Cochrane, Kathy. "Oodgeroo's Journey from Island Dreamtime." *Weekend Australian* 18-19 Sep. 1993: 11.

Collins, John. "Oodgeroo of the tribe Noonuccal." *Race & Class* 35.4 (1994): 77-87.

"A Life Committed to Equality." *Australian* 17 Sep. 1993: 2.

"For Oodgeroo, the Dawn Is at Hand." *SMH* 17 Sep. 1993: 19.

"The 'Fringe Dweller' Who Won World Literary Acclaim." *Age* 17 Sep. 1993: 11.

Kennedy, Fiona. "Nation Mourns Tenacious Mother Figure." *Australian* 17 Sep. 1993: 2.

"A Pioneer of Black Activism and Arts." *Australian* 17 Sep. 1993: 14.

Roberts, Greg. "The Struggle Goes On." *Bulletin* 5 Oct. 1993: 32-35.

Robinson, Judy. "Oodgeroo: A Passionate Voice We Needed to Hear." *SMH* 17 Sep. 1993: 1.

Shoemaker, Adam. "Oodgeroo 1920-1993." *ABR* 156 (1993): 4.

"UNSW Mourns Loss of Aboriginal Educator." *Uniken* 15 (1993): 2.

Walker, David. "The Last Poem of Oodgeroo." *Age* 17 Sep. 1993: 5.

Wright, Judith. "Final Stanza in the Life of Pioneering Poet." *Australian* 17 Sep. 1993: 1.

NOTE

1 I am grateful to Allan Gardiner for his contribution of unpublished bibliographic material to this project. Thanks also to Fryer, Central and Audiovisual Library staff at the University of Queensland for advice and interest.

Notes on Contributors

ULLI BEIER is the Director of the Centre for Modern Art from Africa and the Third World, University of Bayreuth (Germany). He initiated and edited *Quandamooka: The Art of Kath Walker* (1985).

ANNE BREWSTER teaches Creative Writing in the School of Communication and Cultural Studies at Curtin University. Her writing and research interests are in the fields of fictocriticism, Aboriginal women's writing, feminism and postcolonialism. She is currently completing a book on postcolonial literatures for Melbourne University Press.

JOHN COLLINS came to publishing after teaching in secondary schools in Australia and England and at the Universities of Melbourne and of the South Pacific. He was Managing Director of Jacaranda Press and then of Jacaranda Wiley from 1974 until 1993.

RHONDA CRAVEN shared a unique relationship with Oodgeroo. Rhonda is a teacher educator at the University of New South Wales where she continues to ensure Oodgeroo's work lives on in the hearts and minds of student teachers. She is also the project co-ordinator for the national teachers' project initiated by Oodgeroo, as well as an executive member of the Aboriginal Studies Association and a founding member of the Oodgeroo Trust.

ALAN DUNCAN, a retired teacher and academic, has been involved in the Aboriginal rights movement and in Aboriginal education for more than forty years. He was on the executive of the Federal Council for the Advancement of Aborigines and Torres Strait Islanders (FCAATSI) during the 1960s and was the NSW Chairman of the 'Vote Yes' Committee for the 1967 Referendum. Alan initiated Leadership Training courses and Community Development programs for adult Aboriginal people. He then introduced the Aboriginal Family Education Centres and in 1974 designed the very successful Aboriginal Teaching Assistants program at the University of Sydney. Oodgeroo often commented that Alan taught her a lot about Aboriginal culture and Aboriginal pride and that he made many personal sacrifices for her people. She classed Alan as one of her best friends.

EVE FESL is a member of the Gubbi Gubbi clan (maternal) and Gangalu clan (paternal). She was the first indigenous Australian to receive a PhD (1990) and is currently Associate Professor in the Education Faculty at Griffith University, Queensland. Although she has written many papers and articles, it was not until 1993 that her first book, *Conned*, was published by UQP. This dealt with the power of language to oppress her people and how English was used to maintain a conspiracy of silence about the activity of slavery in Australia.

BOB HODGE is Professor of Humanities at the University of Western Sydney, Hawkesbury; co-editor with Jack Davis of *Aboriginal Writing Today* and co-author with Vijay Mishra of *Dark Side of the Dream*.

PAT JARVIS, FAY RICHARDS and EDNA WATSON are sisters from the Darug community in Sydney. Pat, Fay and Edna are Aboriginal culture educators who teach their language and their culture in schools and universities in the Sydney region. Oodgeroo valued the work of these women and attended many Darug functions to support and promote the Darug community.

NICHOLAS JOSE, writer, was Cultural Counsellor at the Australian Embassy, Peking 1987-1990. He is co-translator with Sue Trevaskes of *The Finish Line: A Long March by Bicycle through Australia and China* by Sang Ye (UQP, 1994). His fourth novel *The Rose Crossing* is also due in 1994.

JANINE LITTLE is a postgraduate studying Murri, Koori and Nyoongah women's narrative at the English Department, University of Queensland.

PHILIP McLAREN, born in Sydney in 1943, is a proud descendant of the Kamilaroi people from the Warrumbungle Mountain area in northwestern New South Wales. He has produced, written, directed, and designed programs for major television networks. Today he writes full time, and lives in Sydney with his wife and two children. In 1993 he published the Unaipon Award winning *Sweet Water — Stolen Land* (UQP).

MUDROOROO, poet, novelist, and critic, is one of the leading contemporary Aboriginal writers and spokespersons. He is well known for his novels, including *Wild Cat Falling* (1965), *Doctor*

Wooreddy's Prescription for Enduring the Ending of the World (1983), *Doin' Wildcat* (1988), *The Kwinkan* (1993); poetry, *The Garden of Gethsemane* (1991) and a critical book, *Writing from the Fringe* (1990).

LUCY PETTIT is Oodgeroo's oldest sister and a respected Elder of the Noonuccal tribe. She has shared her experiences of Oodgeroo's formative years, having had a close relationship with her sister over a 72-year period. Lucy continues to ensure her sister's wishes are enacted by contributing to the maintenance and promotion of Noonuccal culture in her role as a Noonuccal Elder and in serving as a member of the Oodgeroo Trust. Oodgeroo greatly respected her sister Lucy and we value her contribution to this book.

EVA RASK KNUDSEN is the author of *Tilbage til fremtiden: australsk aboriginal litteratur siden 1964* (Back to the Future: Australian Aboriginal Literature since 1964) and a number of articles on Aboriginal writings in English. She spent one year at Sydney University under the Australian-European Awards Program. She is a lecturer in the English Department of Odense University in Denmark and is now finishing a project comparing Aboriginal and Maori writing.

SUE RIDER is a theatre director, actor, playwright, dramaturge and teacher, with experience in mainstream, community and educational theatre. She has worked in the UK and Nigeria and, since 1975, in Australia. She is currently Artistic Director of La Boite Theatre in Brisbane.

ADAM SHOEMAKER is the Canadian-Australian author of *Black Words, White Page* (UQP, 1989) and *Mudrooroo* (Collins/A&R, 1993); he also co-edited the first national anthology of Black Australian writings, *Paperbark* (UQP, 1990). He teaches in Australian Studies at the Queensland University of Technology.

ANGELA SMITH is Director of the Centre of Commonwealth Studies, University of Stirling, and is President of the British Australian Studies Association.

ROBERTA SYKES is Senior Lecturer at the Aboriginal Research and Resource Centre at the University of New South Wales, and Founder/Executive Officer of Black Women's Action in Education Foundation.

ROBERT TICKNER is the Federal Minister for Aboriginal and Torres Strait Islander Affairs.